Michael John Pole was born in Auckland, New Zealand. On completion of his college education, he worked briefly for the New Zealand Broadcasting Corporation, then travelled overseas. During this period, his interest in photography developed.

After his overseas sojourn, he worked in a creative capacity for an advertising agency on his return. Eventually, he would establish his own commercial/advertising photography company which he ran for thirty years. Clients included major brands and agencies such as BMW, Toyota, Kodak, Saatchi, JWT, banks, insurance and airline companies. Work commitments took him to Europe, USA, Asia and the Pacific. After the author and work colleagues survived a light plane crash in December 1997, he came to know Christ. In later years, he was invited to serve on the board of the Ruel Foundation which he and his wife, Linda, actively support. In 2011, the family moved (with Sam) to Queensland, Australia, where they still reside today.

For my sister, Julie Hambling, who spent many years praying I would know the Lord. For my wonderful wife, Linda, and children, Talia and Jason, who have supported my career choices without question.

Michael John Pole

SAM AND THE OPEN ROAD

AUSTIN MACAULEY PUBLISHERS™
LONDON • CAMBRIDGE • NEW YORK • SHARJAH

Copyright © Michael John Pole 2023

The right of Michael John Pole to be identified as author of this work has been asserted by the author in accordance with sections 77 and 78 of the Copyright, Designs and Patents Act 1988.

All rights reserved. No part of this publication may be reproduced, stored in a retrieval system, or transmitted in any form or by any means, electronic, mechanical, photocopying, recording, or otherwise, without the prior permission of the publishers.

Any person who commits any unauthorised act in relation to this publication may be liable to criminal prosecution and civil claims for damages.

The story, the experiences, and the words are the author's alone.

A CIP catalogue record for this title is available from the British Library.

ISBN 9781398470903 (Paperback)
ISBN 9781398470927 (ePub e-book)
ISBN 9781398470910 (Audiobook)

www.austinmacauley.com

First Published 2023
Austin Macauley Publishers Ltd®
1 Canada Square
Canary Wharf
London
E14 5AA

Paul the Apostle wrote in Corinthians we must celebrate the contribution of others in life, as the key to any team is its diversity of skills. *Sam and the Open Road*, as a project, has required assistance and encouragement from others in the development of the manuscript.

Dr John Douglas (MA, D. Min), pastor and friend, spent considerable time critiquing the doctrine of this book, while my niece, Rebecca Hambling (BA English/History, Grad Dip Sec Teaching) played a considerable part in the initial editing process. Barry Morris (B. Psych (Hons)) took time out from his busy schedule to review and share ideas regarding whom this book may help and bless.

David and Linda Cowie, mission trips to Fiji and the Philippines with you allowed me to develop valuable insights for God's requirements and the practical application of Christianity for day-to-day living. Your example of commitment in ministry being invaluable, as were your reviews and comments of the script.

To friends, Mike and Nikki Pierce, Chris Souness, Stuart and Gaye Causer, Geoff and Julie Hambling, John and Kaye your spiritual support and thoughts after reading the rough draft spurred me on to conclude this literary journey.

'Sam' represents something uniquely left field in creation. This rather scruffy New Zealand Heading Dog with a heart of gold and mighty spirit to match, found farm life was not for him. Graeme Merchant, who at that time, was Sam's owner, gifted him to my son, Jason. Over time, our engaging new family member became a constant companion. Graeme thank you for Sam. Who would ever have thought he would end up in a book!

Endorsements

Mike, your whole is grounded on the theology of God's being, character, person and Divine realness as Trinity and persons. It's theology of Jesus, His relationship to redemption, human belief, regeneration, faith, spiritual (Christlike) formation, and mission are clearly defined, applied and integrated. Your work addresses the what and how of God's presence acts in His 'saving faith and one's following Christ faith'. The whole work addresses the why, what and how of following Jesus in daily life and purpose – You and Sam are helpful guides and mentors!!!

– John C. Douglas
(MA. D. Min)

This book beautifully integrates two very important elements that we all need for an effective and meaningful life. Firstly, a comprehensive and insightful understanding of the harsh realities and dilemmas we will face. Secondly, the presence of a faithful friend to share our burdens, to be present through the highs and lows, and to help us hold on to hope.

If you have spent any time considering your purpose in life, and this has raised more questions than answers, this book may be your missing piece. Michael has found a way to break down the complexity of our life journey into a collection of simple, yet powerful reflections, aided by his long journey in both following Jesus, and spending a lifetime with a man's (other) best friend!

For those who want to lead an intentional life from the beginning—this book is for you. For those who find themselves lost in mid-life, and need to recalibrate and refocus—this book is for you. For those who want to impart knowledge and wisdom on the generations that will come after you—this book is for you.

In an age where we spend little time sitting at the feet of our older generations to hear stories and draw from their wisdom, Michael has found a way to share his reflective wisdom, so that his God-given inspiration can be shared beyond his children and their children. As a Psychologist working with youth and emerging adults, I am excited about the potential of this as a guide, a challenge, and an encouragement, to a generation who need it more than ever.

– Barry Morris
Psychologist [B. Psych (Hons)]

"Life is a journey that takes us down uncertain roads. Michael Pole takes you as the reader with him and his friendly pooch Sam, on their daily walk as they journey through life's ups and downs. This book will touch you when you least expect it, a read that mixes humour and deep reflection seamlessly to create a reading experience that will resonate with any reader. I can't recommend it more highly."

– Rebecca Hambling
(BA English /History, GradDip Sec Teaching)

I loved this book! Michael Pole paints a picture of his life with his dog, Sam. Each chapter has a delightful story of life with wise insight into the challenges we all face in our human journey. Michael's illustrations out of history and accompanying quotes leaves the reader with much food for thought. This book needs to be read a chapter a day as the sun rises or sets so you can fully enjoy the journey with Michael and Sam and the nuggets of wisdom they both offer to us all.

– David Cowie
Co-Founder Marine Reach

This creatively written book will inspire Christians to love God more deeply and to hunger for greater intimacy with Him. Michael illustrates the awesome privilege of continually walking in the spirit and of hearing his voice at all times. The description of the dawns and sunsets along his 7000km journey are captivating and lead us to a deeper worship of the creator. The anecdotes shared are thought provoking and provide wisdom and words of advice as they touch on life's pertinent issue. You'll also fall in love with faithful Sam… a dog who loves unconditionally and most certainly has enjoyed this journey with his master.

I wish to endorse this book and highly recommend you read it, savour it, go back to the topics from time to time, search out their truths and enjoy.

– Linda Cowie

"I was really looking forward to reading Michaels book and once finished was so thankful that I did."

"The book had me questioning faith and what it meant to me personally. Michael takes you through wonderful journey with Sam, his faithful dog relating experiences and examples of guidance in his life that everyone can relate to. Loved the book and highly recommend It. An excellent read.

– Chris Souness
Nexus Australasia
A division of Souness Developments Ltd.

Table of Contents

Introduction	15
Foreword	17
Sacrifice	20
Attitude	25
Mission	33
Defined or Refined	39
Freedom	45
Faith or Fear	54
Disengage	59
One Blue Eye	65
Within	69
Restoration	75
Bridges	81
Endurance	88
A Reason for Each Season	93
Why Are You Here?	99

An Eagle's Perspective	104
The Thin Blue Line	110
Your Seed Your Legacy	115
Who Is the Master?	121
On a Hill Far Away	127
Sam's Paintbox	132
Once a Story Is Told It Can but Grow Old	138
The Distance Between Us	144
A Certain Place	150
Message in a Bottle	156
Travel with Your Bags Packed	162
In a Word	167
A Wisp of Smoke	174
On the Way Home	179
Eye of the Spirit	185
The Open Road	189
Epilogue	195
Bibliography	197

Introduction

If you do not know the living God and are searching, seeking answers, a first important step is to borrow or obtain a bible. Check out your circle of friends, neighbours and work colleagues, and if they are followers of Jesus take time to hear what they have to say. Start your research, read and learn about Gods love for all his creation and plans He has for you through the lens and promises of scripture. Through Christ, God is the love, hope and truth for all mankind.

What you will learn is not complicated, and should be kept that way. God created you in His image and then sent His Son, Jesus, to earth where he died on the cross for your sins and then he rose again. Jesus now sits at the right hand of God in heaven. Both, God the Father and the Son desire a relationship with you. Jesus, in his infinite grace sent the Holy Spirit when he died, to comfort, council and guide you during life's journey on earth.

Consider God the Father, Jesus the Son and the Holy Spirit as a triangle. Just as water may also appear as liquid, steam or ice, it is still water in different forms. God has simply come in three forms; but they are all one.

- **God:** creator, ruler of heaven and earth, also known as the LORD of Lords and KING of kings.
- **Jesus:** Son of God, sent to earth as man and died for our sins.
- **Holy Spirit:** Helper, guide, comforter, councillor, left with us after Jesus death.

This book intends to mesh world events, biblical and secular, into the patterns of our lives in today's world. As mankind continually repeats events from history our foundation in Christ is vital for our direction and future.

If you have read this far, thank you for considering *Sam and the Open Road* as potential reading and learning material.

Michael and Sam

Foreword

One blue and one brown eye, glossy black coat, white underbelly, splashes of tan and a white stripe atop his head with another running down his neck, completes the picture of Sam. This New Zealand Heading Dog's urban and happy persona created a most endearing image. Sam's farming career as a working dog had stalled, and after a further six months of work experience his previous owner gave up and Sam came to live with us. Legend has it, the farmer was left stranded with stock continually, while Sam headed back to the farmhouse for a cool drink and a snooze under a shady tree. Not a smart career move for a farm dog.

His dissimilar eye colouring (don't worry his sight is perfect) endeared adults and children to him. During the hot summer months, bowls of water from neighbours would magically appear for Sam along with occasional food treats, as we walked.

Whenever you travel the road with others, spiritual bonds are formed with the facets of the relationship becoming burnished and refined. My journey, although about Sam and his adventures, is a stepping-stone, to connect my experiences and time on The Open Road with our Lord and the Holy Spirit, with you.

Bondage in older civilisations were no different than today's yoke of debts, corporates and dependence on nanny states. Politically correct attitudes support culprits and condemn victims with our speech having to fit the left bias. Common sense cannot be found anywhere because it is no longer common and appears to have left years ago. Our minds, young and old, are saturated with reality TV, conflicts and disasters. Our living rooms become a world stage in addition to our phones and computers. Sensationalism has taken media reporting to new levels to maintain ratings and impartiality appears to be a truth from the past.

Many would have to agree, Christian or not, the above imposes additional doubt and anxiety on people's already highly stressed lives. Should we and our families buy into the current worldly offerings without an ability to disengage, the diminishing quality of life will continue to escalate. Freedom of the spirit is not escapism from the above; it is very real and tangible. Your spirit and mine belongs solely to each individual and above all to Him who created us. Spiritual freedom requires only your invitation for our Lord to be part of your life, and through the following chapters, I hope to encourage you on this journey.

After sharing with, close friends and missionaries, David and Linda Cowie about the Holy Spirit's prompting in my life, Linda asked if I was making notes. Would I consider writing a book? Ten months later, the demanding task was underway, fully aware of my literary boundaries, realising I was only a 'co-author'. My walks involved prayer for certain topics, reading the scriptures and praying in the spirit. Certain scripture came alive on the page and the life utilisation either current or historical was prompted by the Holy Spirit.

All promptings are presented as sincerely and accurately as I remember. Often, due to information overload, I had to freehand making rough notes to digest over several weeks. Please understand my prompting was the Holy Spirit, the small clear voice many Christians experience. I am confident, however, this book has been written with heartfelt sincerity to encourage others who know Jesus Christ or may even be searching. My hope and prayer for you is to approach the Lord confidently and at such a personal level as I have done.

Through the following chapters I seek to mesh historical, personal, and world events with a kingdom that is so near and yet appears so far, when this need not be the case. 'Our Lord' is a relational God with scripture in both Old and New Testament, testifying to His desire for every man, woman and child to be relational with Him. Sunday attendance and observation of the Sabbath is important to give praise and to learn. Reading and consuming scripture is vital to opening doorways to your ongoing relationship with Him and to grow. Above all do we set aside time in life's busy schedule to know Him, seeking answers to life's challenges and rejoicing at His presence and wisdom and building on this relationship?

'For we are His purpose
We are His intended
And His purpose
Must always be our intention'.

Sacrifice

> "Anything of value in life has a price
> and will require commitment."

SACRIFICE:

Sam's name to me is an acronym, S(sacrifice), A(attitude), M(mission), the keys and pillars that embody our way of life and the way we choose to live it. Sacrifice is the process of giving up something of value for something worthier. For any of us to achieve and grow, we need to be prepared to sacrifice to reach the goal ahead. Whatever you decide, plan a trip overseas, purchase your own home or plan for your children's future, sacrifice is the embodiment of the process.

The one thing we can never get back in this life is time and the expression seize the day sums it up. You have been given this day so maximise it. This is one day that will never return. The clock cannot be wound back for a re-run; it has been and gone. Time is priceless, so when given to others, it is one of the greatest gifts you can bring to them. When we take time to listen to and hear someone else's story or write a reference that will bless and give opportunity, we are being sacrificial of one of our greatest assets, time.

Sacrifices will come in all shapes, sizes and styles, and all will impact our time in some way, most likely when we least want them to. They ask us to give up that game of golf or leave the surfboard on top of the car rack. Your neighbours may need help in the pouring rain with something that has fallen into the swimming pool during the summer storm. More often than not, 'sacrifices' decide to turn up when you have either the least time available or it is the last thing you want to schedule into your week. If 'sacrifice' was easy, we would see more of it, which is why we don't. When we put the self to one side and be selfless, we extend grace, we move to another room in life by placing others first.

Time spent with our children, where they see sacrificial time in your life, will impact them forever. They will learn giving up is necessary to go up in life; sacrifice is not only voluntary; it is intentional. We identify what we are giving up and accept the price. When we choose to accept the price, part of all sacrifice, either great or small, we intentionally care, have compassion and courage placing others' needs before our own.

In the process of seizing the day or setting goals, all great and positive traits, we cannot forget others who also have dreams and aspirations. You have worked hard for your achievements through study and training for your business, career or sport. All having required a sacrifice of both your time and money. I would like you to consider the journey not only you have made for these goals but also the sacrifices of others, those close to you. They are also part of the sacrifice to help you attain these achievements. Collateral damage with relationships, unfortunately, can be part of goal setting when the result is all-consuming, thereby diminishing the value of your sacrifice. A very clever TV advertisement was created around a man's funeral and you were granted a snapshot of this guy's life. His wedding day, having a family, his Saturday sport, occupation and challenges en route. Beautifully directed and executed, it was a fast forward of a person's life and a scenario familiar to many. Our hero of the advertisement has a large black handlebar moustache, typifying his character. In one scene, he is playing Saturday football heading for a touchdown and at the last second passes the ball to his friend, thereby letting him take the ball over the line. He could have easily scored and taken the glory himself; instead, he passed the opportunity to a friend. Our closing curtain shows an overflowing church, people young and old, all wearing, in tribute, handlebar moustaches. A beautiful idea and example of giving up to go up. How often do we take the ball across the line ourselves when we can easily pass the glory to others?

Anything of value in life has a price and will require commitment if you are to gain it and retain it. Commitment is when you count the cost and keep going, irrespective of discouragements that occur on the journey. Personal let downs, financial losses and endless hours to see light at the end of the tunnel will deter the faint of heart. What you dream to build generally is not a business model befitting your bank or accountant's criteria, as theirs are built on history. At the moment, your idea or venture does not have a history and opposition in the early stages of your plans will either deter you or spur you on to even greater commitment to the race before you. Above-normal success will have always had above-normal opposition and disappointment.

So we set aside things that are of importance to us, withholding personal gratification in the present, so investments in time and energy now benefit our future. The process of sacrifice and self-discipline also changes us. We will not be the same as when we first started, as ongoing development during the journey prepares us for something greater. All due to previous challenges and risks experienced.

Placing others' interests before your own sets valuable precedents and examples to others. Some years ago, a medical mission's ship required a new freezer system. Not only did they require financial assistance for the new freezer, the old one had to be removed first. Being in the bowels of the ship made this a challenging task. Pieces were removed bit-by-bit chain gang style to the dockside rubbish skip. Jason, my son, not even a teenager at the time, assisted me and many other volunteers with the project. To this day, he is a man who will help others at the expense of his own time and energy. When we sacrifice, we also bond, building bridges and relationships, sometimes where there have been none. Emphasis on this word 'sacrifice' cannot be overrated, for the more we place on it, the greater this miracle word becomes.

With sacrifice comes courage and commitment to whatever your dream, vision for your company, the goals of your life and desiring the best for your family under any circumstance. Things you cannot change are called facts, but through sacrifice, you will not be held back and move forward, making all things possible. Having read of incredible sacrificial acts from the corridors of history, you realise these people stand out as they give up to go up. There are also many unsung heroes as well, the mums of this world, who devote themselves to their children, families and home (my wife

Linda) with their never-ending endeavour. Grace is the by-product of sacrifice; through your self-denial grace is extended to others as another was extended to you two thousand years ago for all of mankind.

Sacrifice relinquishes rights and extends grace, just as Jesus did for us. Sometimes, we can be asked to do this under circumstances that are costly to ourselves, but not in either time or monetary terms. Speaking up for an unpopular work colleague or friend at school and knowing when you do, there will be a price. Pontius Pilate had that opportunity and 'washed' his hands of it because he did not believe the Son of God was worth his career. The price of sacrifice is a calculation some do not bother making either out of obedience, love or both. Jesus loved the Father and was obedient to Him and the Father loves us through His Son.

"My Father, if it is possible may this cup be taken from me. Yet not as I will, but as you will." (Matthew 26:39 NIV).

God gave up his Son because He would not put a price on either you or me.

Attitude

"The most subtle attitude change will have multiple knock-on effects."

ATTITUDE:

People love Sam, his demeanour and attitude melts a person's heart when they meet him, he is a reflection of those around him. Total strangers comment, 'Isn't he beautiful', or, 'Look at his eye; is he blind?' No, he is not blind; he has one blue eye and one brown eye. You could call him 'debonair', for Sam is not that young, with frosting around the ears and head, foxy looks and a gentle smile he always wins friends. His body language is down to a fine art; the world falls at his feet and he falls on his feet. Our furry friend is a natural icebreaker and knows how to work the room.

Some time back, I was given a book by Lee Iacocca, past President of Ford and General Motors. In his book, Iacocca mentions receiving a birthday cake from the cleaning lady at the head office, and in return, he extends a personal invitation for her to lunch with him in his presidential office. Many executives and middle management would have killed for that opportunity and no doubt there would have been many discussions around the water coolers. This event shows the genuine down-to-earth value the President of Ford placed on people and he took the opportunity to set an example to management. His is an attitude of caring for all people irrespective of their position or education, illustrating a dynamic leader who leads by service. I can envisage the scene now, worlds apart in both circumstances – income and position – yet sharing lunch, discussing family and touching on things in the company and other interests in life.

Our attitude towards others in life and the world, in general, is shaped by events, both good and bad, and general living experiences. Our experience of others is very much what they experience with us – they reflect who we are. As Sam constantly receives love and adoration, he is only receiving what he is passing on to others. We don't get it right all the time. I know I don't. My expectations of others can sometimes be too high, or we are so concerned about something, we appear blunt or overly direct. Events and circumstances affect our feelings, and these change our attitudes. Instead of going off feelings, go off facts; your feelings will not change the facts no matter how hurt you have been or what you think of yourself. If you consider yourself a failure, that is a feeling, not a fact and that can be changed when the attitude changes. There will be many things you take for granted and most likely do well, but have placed little value on them. They are all important being the starting point of your successes to date; they are not the end game. Should your cup be only half-full, remember there is still something in the cup. Fear of failing can also leave us in our 'failed state' for fear is an emotion and it takes courage, a courageous attitude, to overcome fear.

When we say fear is overcome, it may always be present, but through attitude change, we place fear under control. We move forward and people will see the difference and positive results will be reflected in our lives.

In Biblical scripture, *Joshua 1*, God speaks of not being 'discouraged'. A word describing emotions of concern, loss of confidence, and weakening, but through Me, you will have the courage and I will help you deal with these circumstances. You will have hurdles, such as the course of life itself, even when the Lord is in the midst of it all. Hills and mountains, we have to cross, will not magically disappear but let us change our attitude knowing He is in the centre of all and you walk this road together.

Desire to change attitude is both an intentional and conscious choice and when supported by positive action can help 'reboot' mental change. Should a person decide to reach out and help others, their assistance given to others is often of more benefit to themselves than to those they are helping. A person's attitude will commence to change when you seek why you do certain things a certain way and question them and also when personal accountability comes into the equation. You desire, by conscious choice, to handle situations differently, even if your nemesis reaches out to you again. Continue to be intentional and consciously practice doing this.

This is not about having or maintaining a 'winner's attitude', which seems rather glib, as this does not mean we choose to include in our attitude compassion, generosity, and kindness. On the contrary, this type of attitude, can be one of self-centredness and entitlement that embraces much of today's thinking in professional sports and workplace environments. When we replace the word attitude with gratitude, we will view what the world offers from a different perspective. Both grace and gratitude have the same Greek root (Charis and Eucharistia, respectively) choosing to be grateful for what we do have, appreciating the grace extended to us and so the attitude change commences. Determination, desire to achieve and goal setting are vital; however, if completely unfettered, the winners 'take all' attitude can also take out the winner in the long term.

The subtlest attitude change will have multiple knock on effects in your daily life as people around you at home and the workplace don't just see you; they see the attitude as strangers do when they meet Sam. Some years ago, on a large overseas photography project, my crew and I arrived exhausted at our hotel accommodation. We were ready for a meal and to get much-needed sleep due to the next day's early start and testing schedule. The room was not ready! We had endless cases of equipment on trollies that had to be prepped for the next day's production and all I could think of was food, a call to Linda and sleep. I was tired and not a happy camper. The young lady handling the check-in was struggling to get things underway and I was a little short with her and the way the hotel had handled our bookings. When I finally got to my room settled in, I had second thoughts about my attitude. She had truly extended grace to me and done more than her best under the circumstances, a sudden and humbling realisation. Heading back downstairs, I approached the lobby counter and she appeared not to be there. I asked one of the guys and he said she was just out the back in the office. When she came out, I am certain from her expression she thought this was not going to be good. Introducing myself, I apologised for my attitude and told her it was uncalled for, irrespective of the room issue, which she had handled very well under the circumstances. A beautiful beaming Fijian smile lit her face; grace is very humbling even when booking hotel rooms.

People who have experienced tragedy and terrible grief become weakened spiritually as nothing will compensate and eventually that sadness can turn to bitterness if care is not taken. This will take precedence over our emotions. Business and project failures with long-term financial effects can quickly overpower us if we let them, turning to bitter fruit for those involved or responsible for negative financial outcomes in our lives.

When tragedy involves the loss of a child through unforeseen circumstances, misadventure or illness, the grief process may turn to anger and bitterness, creating a void in our hearts that is impossible to fill. We are then truly vulnerable. In countries around the world, we see monuments, buildings or 'follies' built by people in the hope of overcoming feelings of loss that have engulfed them. The Taj Mahal is one such building commissioned in 1632 by Shah Jahan (Mughal Emperor) after his wife died in childbirth. Twenty thousand artisans were required to complete the project, then the Shah was overthrown by his son and spent the remainder of his life in prison. His only view of the Taj Mahal from his place of incarceration was through a tiny window with the use of a mirror. One of the Seven Wonders of the World, although a masterpiece, represents one tragedy after another and a dysfunctional family where sons and fathers seek to destroy each other for power. Trying to replace painful experiences with material things will never supply the peace required to move on and lead a productive life;

consolation will be temporary and soon be replaced with the same familiar feelings.

Bitterness will sap us like a disease and will not allow circumstances to be put to rest and you cannot because it is spiritual. Eventually, we will express this in the way we speak, with our profanities, harsh and haughty words, all extensions of frustration and resentment fermenting inside.

My genuine belief that the only way to take control is to seek the power of Christ's love for you and let His spirit replace the voids in your life. Should you choose this path, it may happen overnight; it may take years – but in His timing, it will happen and will be ongoing. Any necessity for you to shoulder burdens by yourself will be taken from you, replacing your existing coping mechanisms (anger, anxiety, sadness, esteem) with a reliance on Christ. Old wounds will surface, but this time they will be healed, and the scars will reflect the power and glory of God in your life. For some people, this could be a step into the unknown, a big ask, and every person's experiences of tragedy, loss and disappointment will differ. But why just cope when you can live?

Should you be a Christian and reading this, we know our attitude has to be Christ-centred, and when we work in our strength to make adjustment we are also unconsciously trying to outdo the work that God wants to complete in us. It is a paradox, but the change is completely spiritual.

So, what if you do not follow Christ? I ask you to give serious consideration to completing an Alpha Course (www.alpha.org) and learn about Jesus of Nazareth who changed the world and we are still talking about Him today. All attitudes are internal, some learned behaviour and very often this creates incorrect coping skills when faced with specific circumstances. With the subtlest change in attitude, you will rethink how you do or approach everyday life at home and in the office. Very often, as in all things, correction and adjustment are required to keep us on a fruitful and productive path in life.

Attitudes of entitlement are today's greatest challenges to both the workplace and families. The 'title' does not spell entitlement; but pre-empts the service to those to whom they have an immediate responsibility. Recognising people have human rights is not the issue; understanding there is also an attachment of personal responsibility to those rights and influence. A free lunch is never free; what you may want will always cost. Maybe taking longer, loss of social life, whatever it is, you are the only person who can decide. This is the difficulty with entitlement as it accepts no responsibility, commits to nothing and is about the self. Sadly, it is becoming the figurehead of our society, governments and general thinking. Excellence is the result of attitudes founded in commitment and humility, whereas entitlement creates no value as it is valueless in itself.

Small planes have a device called a 'trim tab', a small wheel in the cockpit the pilot adjusts until the attitude of the aircraft is neutral, thereby keeping the pressure on the controls to a minimum. We are not too dissimilar and as with the trim tab, the smallest attitude change creates large shifts in our lives as in the aircraft. In Luke 9:46-48, we read, *An argument started among the disciples as to which of them would be the greatest. Jesus, knowing their thoughts, took a little child and had him stand beside him. Then he said to them. "Whoever welcomes this little child in my name welcomes me; and whoever welcomes me welcomes the one who sent me. For it is the one who is least among you all who is the greatest".*

Jesus is all things; every day he is also our attitude adjustment as he was to his disciples.

Mission

> "To maintain momentum in whatever we do,
> a clear vision is essential."

MISSION:

In Sam's mind, the bare necessities of life are food, rest, fun and family affection. The mission in Sam's life is built around a natural aptitude to work (I didn't say he was good at his job!). His breeding being programmed to maintain borders around the livestock. As we have no sheep or cattle on our property in Australia, Sam's inbuilt purpose is directed to other things. Running up and down fence lines when horses in the paddock are being fed, rounding up cats (pathetic), chasing and barking instructions at Zeus (our German Shorthaired Pointer) when the ball is thrown. From Sam's perspective, he has a purpose and mission, and it has been accomplished.

Before any mission, there has to be vision. I guess the vision Sam has is built into his DNA and from that stems the mission. We all need a vision for our future. We attend the education system and from people we come in contact with, our teachers, friends and mentors, we shape a vision for our lives. A vision is something about the future, intangible, built on dreams and self-belief and from this we pick a road and commence the race. You have heard the expression start small, dream big? Well, any vision needs to embrace more than just the material aspects of life; they are important but not the whole answer. When you read about great achievers, you get the low down on the lives, the failures, successes and near misses all in considerable detail. Financial details of their lives are generally not of interest, being secondary to what originally drove them, the obstacles encountered, their resilience and determination to achieve the vision.

To maintain momentum in whatever we choose to do, a clear vision is essential, as many ups and downs will occur en route. Clear pictures of who we are and the path needed to reach the final destination are vital to any planned hike in the woods. Similarly, we need the same for the ventures of life. Vision is the fundamental basis of any purpose in life and from the vision, we will have missions. Vision will keep you on task as not all missions are successful, some are very successful, some average and others fail miserably. Vision will have you plan additional missions irrespective of failures and we need to recognise the importance of how personal relationships are vital to any vision.

Other people's relational involvement and a vision being conveyed are shown clearly when Jesus said, *"Come follow me," (Mark 1:17NIV)* to his prospective disciples, adding further still, *"and I will send you out to fish for people."* Hardened fishermen left their business knowing little of what they would learn or where it would lead, yet with a few simple commanding words, their attention was gained and a vision presented. Your vision also has to impact others and needs to be imparted to them. By illustrating its value as Jesus did with the disciples, they will help you build on what you are doing. You are young and could well be planning additional education for your future and career choice, your vision not embracing the ideals of your parents. A remarkable young woman was faced with such a dilemma; however, she remained true to herself and her calling, often being referred to as The Lady of the Lamp. Florence Nightingale came from a wealthy family and nursing was considered both an uneducated and lowly occupation in Victorian times. Certainly not in keeping with the social standing required of her parents. After refusing a proposal in marriage, she enrolled in nursing school against her parents' wishes. She came to great public attention with her work in the Crimean War, changing and developing sanitation methods, as disease and infection were killing more soldiers than the actual wounds inflicted by the battles. Many others have also chosen paths that at the time may not have appeared to offer the security and standing required by family or society but have succeeded due to the clear vision of who they are and their purpose in life.

A personal conviction has everything to do with vision, as once the mission commences you will need to pick the hills you will die on. On such hills, you will see the value of your sacrifice and develop the attitude required to sustain you during those times. So, why do we bother? Because without purpose, mankind fails and drifts from the proper and sound values of living. Life is no dress rehearsal; neither are your wife nor your children's lives, which you have been entrusted with. Without vision, life will seem pointless. You will go through the mechanics of each day looking for a rainbow to suddenly appear and magically all problems and needs will vanish. People with vision have challenges, problems, sleepless nights and everything else that accompanies goal setting. Vision, however, gives them a future, taking the sting out of the sacrifice and through patience they are eventually rewarded. All people need the strength to follow a vision and remain on a path that is true to themselves and honour those around them. You can follow your vision and believe that collateral damage is part and parcel of the process (mentioned previously), but in this scenario, we are then only sacrificing others instead of ourselves.

The vision communicated properly will keep the missions going and the teams on task. Team building programmes are good, but if the vision is not communicated on a day-to-day basis due to an attitude of management towards the team, you won't have a team. Your mission statement, a management protocol, is only as good as the examples set by the leadership. My involvement with a company allowed me to observe first-hand when leadership is transferred to inexperienced hands and the carnage that can result within four to six months. Product quality and services fail; customers show their loyalty with their feet. Even when advised that their approach needs to change, a lack of teachability restricts their minds and actions. That is why good leaders get their hands dirty at the coal face; they are not above or beyond those that serve them. Leading by example is the greatest communication tool of vision to equip your teams.

So how do you get started with a vision for your life, you may be the greatest centre forward in your soccer team, but someday you will be too old to play, retirement will be forced on you, what then? May I suggest you go to He, who created you early in life and find out what He desires for your life. Your agility, the biomechanics, strength and speed to play as you do are from Him. Blessed are your fingers, hands and mind with the ability to be able to play that musical instrument or save a life with the use of a scalpel. A good place to start is in *Genesis 1:1, In the beginning.* Take a look at the vision God has for humankind. It is vast, and by *Genesis 2:3,* the work to construct our earthly home has been completed. The next step is the relationships with those created in His image.

The old TV series Mission Impossible commences each episode the same way, a brief conveying why the good guys should foil some evil, sinister plot. Instructions followed by a statement *'your mission should you choose to accept it'*. Vision always precedes the mission. God shows his vision for his people in *Numbers 13:2* (NIV), when The Lord told Moses *Send some men to explore the land of Canaan (Israel) which I am giving to the Israelites*. Moses then instructed those participating in the mission to gather information on the quality of the land, the people, unwalled or fortified towns and to bring back samples of fruit and plants. On the completion of their exploratory venture, the team reported: "*We went into the land to which you sent us, and it flows with milk and honey! Here is its fruit" (Numbers 13:26 NIV).* All good news, then some not so good. Some spies report people in the land were huge and the city's well fortified "*We can't attack those people; they are stronger than we are" (Numbers 13:31 NIV).* The recording finally self-destructs along with the vision turning to smoke when they say, "*We seemed like grasshoppers in our own eyes, and we looked the same to them" (Numbers 13:33).*

If you have never felt like this about something, I will be surprised, I have, and the keyword is *'felt'*. Based on feelings of fear, inadequacy and doubt, they thought they knew the minds of the opposition when they didn't even know them! An all-embracing vision for the Israelites' future had been cast by the LORD, the goodness of that promise had been confirmed by research and some challenges had to be overcome to secure it. Simple math says you are more than two-thirds of the way there. Unfortunately, it is not the fortified cities and the size of the current inhabitants who pose the challenge; it is the attitude of the Israelites. This incident amongst God's people developed into a full-scale rebellion occurring when they were already halfway to Canaan (Israel). Normal road trip time in those days for the journey was about two weeks; their attitudes and actions towards God and his anointed leadership pushed this out by forty years.

So close, yet so far.

I have always viewed this scripture and story in today's terms as people's self-destruction of a great vision. Those who rebelled had never entered the vision God had for them and therefore never entered the Promised Land. Over forty years, as a generation, they passed away in the desert, their descendants finally crossing the Jordan River into a land of milk and honey. We also need to consider when our inability to realise 'the vision' may suggest something in our lives may be holding us back, just like the Israelites. Take time and share it with the Lord. You may find you are on task with the vision, but something may need adjusting before the next step. There are no hard and fast answers and as Jesus will never give up on you, don't give up on the vision and be open, always, to new direction from Him.

Defined or Refined

"Great success and achievement, comes
at a great price."

DEFINED OR REFINED:

The rolling thunder and forked lighting have run its course, rain falls in torrents, typical of our storms in the summer season. Sam raises his head from under my office desk; now the noise has subsided. Satisfied it is safe, the worst is over, he stretches and heads to the lounge for the sofa and the TV.

Contrary to Sam's behaviour, American buffalo are unique in their approach to the terrible weather they experience during winter, turning their heads into the blizzard and facing the storm. A remarkable attitude in times of adversity and challenge. All have had 'storms' brew in our lives in the form of health, work, business, personal issues, mistakes we have made; the list goes on. Sometimes, it seems never-ending. Our attitude in such times is crucial and even if the outcome is out of control, our attitude will determine the next steps and how we take them. Life has a habit of throwing curveballs, many from left field and our minds become battlefields with the stress of surmounting situations, all of which when focussed on will cause us to doubt, procrastinate and question why. Some things can be rationalised while others not. We either let these things define who we are or have them refine us.

With many of the people who inspire us, we tend to look at their successful lives and wonder at their courage and dedication, forgetting or unaware what has happened behind the scenes. A young Christian woman, Bethany Hamilton, lost her arm in a shark attack while surfing and returned to the water a month after to the sport she so dearly loved. Over time, she went on to secure many prestigious surfing titles, a truly remarkable and courageous feat under any circumstances, let alone with one arm. Above all, she refused to let a tragic and terrifying event rob her potential in life and what she loved doing. Her courageous story reached the world, showing neither her mind, body nor spirit remained captive to the fear of that terrible accident by returning to the water again.

Stephen Spielberg was rejected twice by the USC film school simply because he wasn't good enough! Although he was denied access to university-level training, which he believed would have enhanced his career, his future as a filmmaker was not defined by this. Possibly, it could have made him even more determined only to be awarded an honorary degree by the USC some years later. Michael Jordan, deemed to be one of the world's greatest basketball players, was cut from his high school basketball team and is quoted saying, "I have missed more than 9000 shots in my career, lost 300 games and when entrusted with the game-winning shot I have missed 26 times. I have failed over and over in my life and that is why I succeed."

Any great success or achievement will come at a great price. Thomas Edison made 10,000 attempts at creating the light bulb, none of which he considered a failure, as he said, "I have not failed but found 10,000 ways that don't work." People exhibiting commitment, determination and courage don't do it from the sidelines as they have to enter the arena. Not always a pleasant or safe place, depending on the circumstances. An accident, financial failure, and let-down you may be turned away; these people are not defined by these events but use the process for refining who they are.

Theodore Roosevelt's great speech, 'The Arena', describes the attitude that accompanies the people who choose to enter it.

It is not the critic who counts; not the man who points out how the strong man stumbles, or where the doer of deeds could have done them better. The credit belongs to the man who is actually in the arena, whose face is marred by dust and sweat and blood; who strives valiantly; who errs, who comes short again and again, because there is no effort without error and shortcoming; but who does actually strive to do the deeds; who knows great enthusiasms, the great devotions; who spends himself in a worthy cause; who at the best knows in the end the triumph of high achievement, and who at the worst, if he fails, at least fails while daring greatly, so that his place shall never be with those cold and timid souls who neither know victory nor defeat.

So, do we turn our heads into the storm or do we walk away? We can stand our ground even with failure looming on the horizon realising accomplishment has a price and it must be paid and without daring, we will accomplish nothing.

In 492 BC, a young Jewish girl of incredible beauty rose from very humble beginnings to the harem of King Xerxes 1, eventually becoming his chosen queen. Hadassah, also known as Esther, was an orphan and her guardian and cousin Mordechai made her promise to keep her Jewish lineage secret from the royal court.

At that time, King Xerxes 1, his power and jurisdiction extended from Lydia to the borders of India, Egypt and Libya. Jewish citizens in these regions had engaged in and maintained peaceable relationships for many years alongside their Persian neighbours. However, politics and events would change with the arrival of Haman, the king's new premier. Ethnic cleansing of all Jews was decreed within Xerxes Kingdom, and prevention of this pending genocide fell upon the young shoulders of Esther, only 14 or 15 years old at that time. Esther, by necessity and being a Jew herself, would have to approach the king in defence of her people when the law stated no person could approach the king's court uninvited. Dangers attached to her courageous decision are apparent in *Esther 4:16 NIV*: "*I will go to the king, even though it is against the law. And if I perish, I perish.*" Esther approached the king uninvited and was accepted; the genocide averted; and the new government law revoked. Due to courage and daring, this young woman stepped into the arena for her people irrespective of life or death consequences. Refusing to be defined by political conditions that would define future outcomes, Esther was refined by her faith and gained considerable credibility in King Xerxes kingdom.

These examples from history and current times show commitment and determination, whatever the situation, they also show great courage. Winston Churchill wrote, *"Courage is rightly considered the foremost of the virtues, for upon it all others depend."* For the values of courage will involve sacrifice and service, family and others first before your desires and wants. When we choose to stand for what is close to our hearts, the arena can be a lonely place often subject to much negativity envy and even ridicule. Whatever our challenges, courage will see that we follow through regardless of the scratches and bruises gained along the way. Each day, we take the next step a new step. This human value is not restricted to battle-hardened soldiers; it is a quality held by mothers for their children. My sister shared about a family in which two boys in their late teens suffered from muscular dystrophy. To alleviate her children's level of pain, she had to turn them every two hours. Totally in tears, exhausted and worried, she rang my sister for prayer. This mother will continue to take the next step, a new step each day.

Our refining takes place in our spirit and our minds; the more we practice dealing with difficult circumstances and believing for positive outcomes, the more we can achieve. For curveball events will no longer be allowed to compromise our potential. There are times we think enough is enough. I am sure you have, and I certainly have experienced that emotion, and that is all it is – an emotion. Let us move beyond this knowing there is a gracious Father in Heaven who treasures His children and we are not to be discouraged in any way but to have courage in all that we do. *"What, then, shall we say in response to these things? If God is for us, who can be against us?" (Romans 8:31 NIV).*

Challenges great and small will always be dished up at work, home, church and schools and going unchecked can define us, but God's Grace will refine us. Our choice now befitting His will, and not conforming to the expectations of the world. Not always easy, for your faith must reach for and embrace wholeheartedly, the important word 'trust'. Paul says in *Romans 12:2 NIV*, *"Do not conform to the pattern of this world, but be transformed by the renewing of your mind."* When we intentionally choose to renew how we deal with certain situations, refining commences in our lives due to His Grace.

Sam's nervous attitude to loud noise, storms and fireworks is fairly typical of his breed; however, in my office, at my feet, he finds courage knowing the storm will move on. He will not be defined by these events, as he would never go outside again. Maybe we should all rest at His feet more often.

Freedom

"The sell-out of our future to our previous poor decision making only happens when we allow our character and thoughts to be defined by what we were."

FREEDOM:

Sam trots ahead of me, head down and unrestrained experiencing the surrounding scents coming from the ground, road markers and trees. History exists in these scents. Those who have been on the path before him, people, friend or foe, a gourmet of smells for his assessment. Although obedient and smart, Sam cannot rationalise as his decisions are predetermined by instinct and breeding.

On the other hand, we can rationalise and make choices. Allowing an additional tier of freedom over and above Sam's on his daily excursions. The downside of our 'free will' is the attached level of responsibility and the corresponding outcome of the choices we make. Poor decisions will ensnare not only ourselves but those close to us, whereas conversely good decisions will benefit. Our ability to assess and respond to certain situations appropriately, however difficult or testing, will create the correct paths for the future. Our choices give us either a free run or many hurdles to overcome in mind, body and spirit.

Many people restricted due to physical infirmity, in general, do not allow this to inhibit their way of life. Nor do they consider themselves disadvantaged. You see this in the Invictus Games competitors. Entrepreneurs with a new start-up business may fail the first, second or third time only to regard their failures as lessons, continuing to try until they eventually succeed. In all of these situations, they have neither permitted their circumstances to decide their future nor to remain bound by them. When Peter and his crew went fishing all night *(John 21.3NIV)*, they were still empty-handed in the morning. Christ called to them from the shore telling them to cast the net on the other side and they almost sank the boat with the number of fish they caught *(John 21.6 NIV)*. The disciples actions were intentional, a simple first step to becoming fishers of men.

In the list of choices available to us, indecision is the close cousin of poor choice serving no one. It will deprive us of any possible achievement, as nothing can be learned from it and time never to be regained, is stolen. Indecision can bind us and show neither trust nor faith due to inaction. If Peter and his crew had chosen not to follow Jesus' instruction, their fishing expedition would have been a waste. Should indecision have ruled, and had they not attended to the command immediately, a positive outcome would not have occurred. Time and again, indecision looms in the choice process for any decision requires commitment. Responsibility and accountability rest with the decision-maker. As poor choices are binding, so is indecision and when the tough calls are not attended to either in your business, organisation or family life, purpose and vision disappear.

Our poor decisions come in many forms where work, money and career are the primary focus or possibly even addictions. Leaving families wondering how it can all be going so wrong. Bumps and knocks on the world's roller coaster will never stop; they are sent to unseat us, and we become reactive instead of acting, commencing the downward spiral. Day by day, the hole we dig for ourselves becomes deeper with minds and spirits settling into some dark space called 'worry' (captivity) and any path to the open road is a dream.

King Zedekiah was advised by Jerimiah, the prophet, to surrender to the Babylonians in *Jerimiah 38:17NIV*. Should they follow Gods instructions Jerusalem's population would then go into captivity; the city would not be ransacked and the lives of the people spared. *"Obey the LORD by doing what I tell you. Then it will go well with you, and your life will be spared" (Jerimiah 38:20 NIV)*. Decisions contrary to God's will meant they would become an object of horror and scorn, previously prophesised in the coming judgment (*Jerimiah 25:8-9 NIV*). Life's options and choices for the people of Jerusalem had been taken from them. Foundations for their pending captivity or survival have been laid through previous poor choices and immoral behaviour. God's hand of Grace was being extended, an opportunity to re-evaluate their lives with the eventual return to Israel some years later was available. A final decision by the Israelites not to surrender was reached due to their failure to see their current situation as a result of previous poor choices. An offer of temporary captivity, a place of adjustment, would ensure a positive outcome, with an eventual return to their homeland. Unfortunately, their lives were lost, and the city was destroyed.

Poor choices will change the road we travel and very often the road is signposted with words such as pride, impulse, selfish convenience, and inexperience. What appears in our homes will very often appear in our workplace or business. Our responsibility is to recognise and deal with these failings, thereby reflecting positive changes in our lives and those around us.

David and his outlawed followers freely assisted a wealthy landowner (Nabal) by protecting his shepherds from bandits and robbers (*1 Samuel 25 NIV)*. However, when David requested assistance for some badly needed supplies, he was rudely denied. His fuse lit, David was now enraged, deciding to take all he required by force. With anger now at the helm, David was about to affect his future ruling as King of Israel. Terrible retribution against him and his followers would definitely follow. Fortunately for David, Abigail, the landowner's wife, got wind of what was on the horizon and moving from the wings she stepped into the scene. Realising the pending disaster, she prepared supplies before courageously riding out to meet David and his men. Appealing to David's better judgment and overriding her husband's foolishness, using wisdom and diplomacy, Abigail diffused the situation and prevented a massacre.

We are not all fortunate enough to have an Abigail on tap pre-empting a poor choice. Both Nabal (Abigail's husband) and David failed to see the 'big picture' and would have ensnared their futures due to pride and poor choices. Nabal and his workers would have lost their lives, David would have blotted his copybook, placing his leadership and fitness to be Israel's future king in question. Fortunately, David was teachable, recognising his poor judgment when presented to him; setting aside his ego and listening *(1 Samuel 25:33 NIV)*. Although King David did not always make wise choices, this was one righteous choice that allowed him to proceed on the path for which he was anointed. Without this brave woman, Abigail, David's story could have been dramatically different.

Somewhere in our lives, we may have sold ourselves cheaply to poor choices, allowing these to determine and decide the course and paths for the future. Very often your last mistake is your next step forward or could we rephrase this and say, *your current challenge is an opportunity to overcome*. The sell-out of our futures to our previous poor decision-making only happens when we allow our character and thoughts to be defined by what we were. Should we intentionally, in heart, mind and spirit, allow previous circumstances to refine us, we will go forward each day with courage into a positive and productive future.

In your home or company are decisions made based on expediency and convenience or are they made with integrity and a desire to serve your family and staff correctly? Decisions made through pride, selfish convenience and expediency, as David did initially, will always produce unsatisfactory outcomes, even if the result is faster and easier. Revealing themselves further down the line in the form of poor family relationships, low-profit margins, high rotation of staff and bad press. To reflect the change, we need to ask, are we doing the same old thing the same old way expecting a different result? Often referred to as the height of insanity. Governments and companies do this all the time, with ambulances racing to the bottom of the cliff with Band-Aids. It is easier and more convenient in their opinion to do this, for through expediency popularity will not be lost. Often, confrontation, never an easy task, is the only solution in these circumstances. Abigail would have had to muster all the courage she had to ride out and meet someone in a male-dominated world who was set on her family's demise. Presenting the situation to David in a humble and forthright manner, with an understanding of the circumstances and future consequences, she painted a memorable picture.

As people, we can change and make better choices by intentionally applying constructive thoughts to our lives and choosing to act on them. Life's foundations need to be set on rock-solid core values; values we are not prepared to compromise for the sake of our self-gain or temporary pleasure. How do our lives line up with those core values? Are our actions a reflection of them? If they don't, then our current circumstances may only change if we choose to realign ourselves with those values.

Operating on forty percent power, with electrical and hydraulic system's failing and jamming most of their guns, an American B17 bomber was returning from Bremen, Germany in WWII. While passing over enemy territory to allied air space, they were observed by a German Luftwaffe air ace (Franz Stigler) whose aircraft was currently being armed and refuelled at a nearby airfield. Once airborne again, the Luftwaffe pilot went in pursuit of the B17, only finding on close inspection the terrible condition of the bomber and its crew. Holes in the B17's fuselage revealed wounded and incapacitated crewmembers struggling for survival. The Luftwaffe pilot indicated for the B17 to follow him to his airbase where the crew could surrender and receive urgent medical attention. Realising the B17 crew was not responding to his request and to prevent German land-based anti-aircraft guns from firing, Stigler courageously flew alongside the crippled B17. When both aircraft reached international waters Stigler saluted them and returned home.

Stigler made a choice based on values he would not compromise. His choice carried the risk of his actions being found out or reported to his commanders and a court-martial was very much on the cards. Overriding values of compassion and integrity would not allow this pilot to dispatch the incapacitated B17 even at the risk of his own life.

Possibly, the amount of numbing destruction and loss of life he had already experienced made this the last straw. Whatever the rationale at the time, he was not prepared to sell out his future due to fear or how he would be regaled by his peers or commanders.

We can be faced with decisions that challenge our foundations and values, not as life and death (as for Stigler) but ask that we go against the tide of opinion and say, "No, that's not happening." The result is often unpopularity with people close to you or a major disagreement due to dishonest dealings by your partners with clients. With anything of true value, there is a price.

Fearing for his life, Peter denied Jesus, not once, but three times at the time of his arrest. One can only imagine from Peter's perspective during this turbulent and political situation the mental challenge he was going through. Unfortunately, as with all of us, doubt showed up and the drop appeared too great. A well-founded fear for the Pharisees and the powers that be at that time became the deciding factor in Peter's choice. His denial must have torn his spirit with self-disappointment, grief and guilt robbing him of so much, yet Jesus healed that. From this terrible place, the brash, loud fisherman from Galilee became empowered with courage, tenderness and uncompromising in his stand for Jesus. Ultimately costing him his life but revered forever in history.

Freedom is spiritual first and foremost. I am sure you have sensed this when experiencing open spaces on a hilltop or the early morning light crossing the waves as you lie on your surfboard, waiting for the first ride of the day. Even though these are physical experiences, they touch us spiritually – I guess that's why we do it to get away from it all. Our coin when tossed, has two sides, one is called captivity and the other freedom. Mortgage sizes and other material gratification are based on pride and self; they are choices. Anyone who works hard should also enjoy the fruits of their successes, but when this becomes all-consuming, you have not created financial freedom, you have now become captive.

Every person's journey is unique, and the guiding principles God has set for a fulfilling and purpose driven life are the same for the non-believer and believer. In *Romans 2:14,* Paul's commentary addresses this:

"Indeed, when Gentiles, who do not have the law, do by nature things required by the law, they are a law for themselves, even though they do not have the law". By virtue of our nature our conscience convict's mankind when we break Gods guidelines.

So why do you need Jesus?

For redemption, accountability, so the Holy Spirit, whom He baptises us with when we accept him into our lives helps us navigate the pitfalls and rocks on the road ahead.

Sam will never understand the wonderful freedom he experiences, for as previously mentioned he can't rationalise. But we can, as God gave us free will.

Faith or Fear

"The LORD himself goes before you and will be with you."
(Deuteronomy: 31:8)

FAITH OR FEAR:

Daisy, the tortoiseshell cat, waits patiently behind the door. Sam is oblivious to her presence, and when the time is right, merciless revenge will be exacted on this unsuspecting canine. This will be punishment (in Daisy's eyes, it's called sport) for rounding her up like a sheep and staring her down with his 'withering gaze'. I open the door to my office and Sam follows me out of habit. Daisy attacks with a hiss and outstretched paw full of claws. Sam, terrified, yelps heading into the office seeking safety under my desk. Daisy satisfied with the level of terror inflected slinks off to another room to contemplate further attacks.

Intimidation is not uncommon in corporate or institutional environments and can force co-workers and colleagues to withdraw due to anxiety, reducing performance levels to the detriment of the organisation. We have all experienced anxiety at times that fill your life with heart-wrenching concern for your health, job, child or finances. For no apparent reason, the commitment and hard work are torn from under your feet at a moment's notice, and like a house of cards, your world appears to be caving in. Anxiety and apprehension can become a default setting, achieving nothing and costing everything. First things to disappear are constructive and rational thinking with problems appearing to follow us in an unsolvable stream. Not for a minute, would I consider the seriousness of health or financial issues something to simply brush off; it is the choices we make and how we choose to go forward that is important. Inside, we feel we have sacrificed enough and the word 'quit' comes to mind. God, however, does not give up on his children easily.

The LORD himself goes before you and will be with you; he will not leave you or forsake you. Do not be afraid; do not be discouraged. (Deuteronomy: 31:8 NIV).

When challenged with adversity, it is instinctive to batten down the hatches, take hold of the reins and subconsciously decide to do it your way. The desire to personally control the situation is an automatic reaction to protect family and yourself, when in fact you need someone to help you navigate the unknown waters ahead. Feelings of helplessness emerge; they are not pleasant when you take on something as major as an insurance company who appears to have the power over your life and your family's wellbeing. You have to pause and realise you need to let *The LORD himself go before you.* Surrender is your part of the process and with the declaration of the power of God, you allow Him to open and close doors. *My Lord come down and take over!* He will guide and steer the course so there is no reason to be fearful or discouraged.

If you truly believe there is a plan for your life, I suggest that you allow the designer of the plan to get on with the job. Unfortunately, human nature is such when times are good 'the plan' is working the way we want it. When times are tough, we tell ourselves, 'This is not what I signed up for'.

Our testing process comes in times of adversity, which in turn will build and shape our character to fulfil what God wants for our future. Bearing in mind, we did sign up to trust God, under *all circumstances* with our lives, families and welfare. When our thinking oscillates, we fluctuate as emotions of worry and fear have been invited to the thought process and our faith disappears. Without a doubt, I am certain you have experienced many difficulties in life and I can assure you I have been in a similar position where my thinking also fluctuated under adverse circumstances. Changes to these situations do not occur overnight and change in our-selves may not always be as rapid as desired, being in His timing, not ours. After receiving the plans and design on how to build the Ark of the Covenant and the Tent of the Tabernacle, the Israelites completed the task and under Moses' leadership followed the instructions to the letter. On completion, *Then the cloud covered the tent of the meeting, and the glory of the LORD filled the tabernacle (Exodus 40:34 NIV). Whenever the cloud lifted from above the tabernacle, they would set out; but if the cloud did not lift, they did not set out – until the day it lifted (Exodus 40:36-37 NIV).* They moved forward in their journey in God's timing, not their own. I know when we rest in His trust and grace, transformations also start to take place. For we allow His work to seed properly and come to fruition.

I planted carrot seeds as a child in my father's garden. Being a naturally impatient nine-year-old when the first green shoots poked their heads up, I pulled up the plant to see if a carrot had grown. I soon learned to leave them alone, give them water and they will grow. Our timing is not part of His process in our journey and if we step in and try to speed things up, we invariably 'mess up' as I did with the carrots.

On first meetings with any person, we have to take time to know them and understand them.

We have been given a manual for understanding who our Father in Heaven is and by reading the scriptures He shares the vision He has for our lives. Similar to receiving overseas mail or emails from people you have not met and a picture starts to build of who they are. No shortcuts are available when getting to know someone; the more time you spend with them and in communication, the more you will understand them. So where do faith and fear come into this picture? When faith is truly at work under any circumstance, fear, discouragement and worry will not find room in our lives. This is due to God's sovereignty, for they have not been permitted to be part of who we are as all permission has been given to God. When you give your surgeon permission to conduct an operation, it is done while you are sleeping. You do not wake up halfway through and say no, I have changed my mind. He has already been granted permission to complete the task in front of him, replace your heart valves, or give you a replacement hip. So how can God do the great work He wants to do in your life if you cancel the permission partway through because something's not happening fast enough? He knows which carrots have grown the most, which have come to maturity and all he wants us to do is water them and thank Him with praise.

Faith is a mighty tool, as Jesus explains in *Matthew 17:20 NIV*: "*Truly I tell you, if you have faith as small as a mustard seed, you can say to this mountain, 'Move from here to there' and it will move. Nothing will be impossible for you*".

Fear is the adrenalin before our natural fight or flight, and God knowing our fear, His courage in us will strengthen us in the face of adversity and we will not be discouraged through faith. Quite different from Sam's confrontations with Daisy! Sometimes we look at others and think they have the 'perfect' life, trouble-free (apparently), and we compare – a dangerous place to go. Later, we realise behind the scenes things have not been that flash with health or business worries, teenage kids giving parents grief. The enemy (Satan) wants you to compare, be discontented and not to believe in the impossible. Kind David wrote, "*You prepare a table before me in the presence of my enemies*" (*Psalm 23:5 NIV*), where our Lord prepares you to 'sit' and face what is before you. Recognise it as the enemies' desire for you to give up and surrender to the anxiety and concerns facing you. God's grace will be upon you and protection will be given and blessed to you in great abundance for "*You anoint my head with oil; My cup overflows.*" Jesus is present at that table, asking us to come and sit with Him, so simple – easy. His anointing comes in the form of healing mind, body and spirit, infirmities and disease. Discouragement is replaced by courage and hopelessness is replaced with faith and trust. Whatever your situation requires, Jesus has an anointing for it.

Disengage

> "Disengage and take the control back
> where it belongs."

DISENGAGE:

Zeus, a highly energetic German Short Haired Pointer, who is well aware of his blue blood and ability to outrun, bark louder (when he considers it required), is also a family member. Both Sam and Zeus will chase the tennis ball in the never-ending game for hours. Sam's working instincts become apparent when he runs and barks beside Zeus, encouraging him to retrieve the ball. When the game has not been played for extended periods, both engage in unsubtle manipulation, nudges on your leg and head resting on your knee. All very obvious, continuing until somebody picks up the ball thrower and engages in the game again.

The word engage refers to actual combat situations as well as seeking to attract the attention of others. Disengage, its antonym, is to remove troops from an area of conflict, or in the sport of fencing to slide the blade of your sword over or under your opponents to change the line of attack. Normally, we are quite relaxed when our interest or attention is gained or engaged by another party, on other occasions not so. Difficulties can arise when we seek to move on from these situations and an option to disengage is not easily conducted, the choice is taken from us a little like Sam and Zeus and their unsubtle manipulation!

People's privacy and the ability to disengage has been seriously compromised by call centres, mobile phones, and information sold between companies without our knowledge. Add to this social media leaks and the information highway is now for sale. Like it or not, you and I are caught in its web. Cold calling insurance companies (total strangers) are asking for our financial details, personal debt levels, and income information. My parents would have never discussed their financial situation with anyone other than their bank and accountant and I will not be drawn into that conversation either.

Our world is faceless and cold. Between colleagues and friends in business, human relationships are pushed into dark corners, where there is no light other than that emanating from the text on their cell phone screen or emails on the computer. People now meet in cyberspace with the rest of the world, becoming the norm for meetings and the forefront of all we do. Our living rooms become the battlefields of far-flung wars on terrorism as media and governments struggle to explain battle lines that are no longer defined and human suffering is sent to us in a numbing sociological palette.

We carry on bravely with the everyday issues of raising families, jobs, mortgages, educating our children and planning for retirement. Psychologists are already pointing at the issues I have mentioned and the impact on today's society; the level of sensationalism is with us 24/7 with no let-up.

Toxic relationships of any kind will eventually force you to disengage for personal health reasons, and each day's current smorgasbord to society by multiple media systems available is total overload, we need to consciously disengage.

David, when on the run from Saul would have felt the pressure and been stressed, as any military leader knowing should he be caught it would end badly for him and his men. A fact he could not change. However, David put his energies into what he could change and control, keeping the enemy at a distance as he did with Goliath, trusting God and working within the boundaries and understanding of what God wanted for him.

"He refreshes my soul" (Psalm 23:3 NIV).

Suggesting, in this time of adversity, his mind was at peace, disengaged from Saul and his army who were beyond the entrance of his cave, David's place of refuge. The worries of this global village will be brought in a never-ending stream to the entrance of your cave in every form of distraction and it is essential we be good gatekeepers of our hearts, minds and homes. Be like David and do not let them in; disengage.

The world wants you to engage at every point and in its own eyes does not believe you have a choice not to. You are sold a perception of who you need to be, and how to succeed believing this will come through appearances, status, awards and accolades – I have been there, we all do it to a degree. Being a good gatekeeper is essential to your process of disengagement and not to be confused with caring or listening. Good gatekeepers protect their hearts and select what they will hear, see and absorb, all of which affect the human spirit. Building walls so we cannot be reached by humanity will only make us ineffective in a world God requires us to be relational in. However, we need to choose carefully and know when to disengage, developing skills to change the battle lines and select the places of confrontation. Some situations will require us to walk away knowing full well a certain relationship, business or person is toxic, meaning time invested will eventually compromise our lives. Jesus has told us under certain circumstances we are to shake the dust off our feet *(Matthew 10:11–14)* and move on. Disengage and take the control back where it belongs with ourselves, for when we choose to battle the enemy at *their* point of conflict, the greater the chance we will work in the flesh (the way of the world) and not the spirit (the way of God).

Recently, I had a business deal 'go south'; three and half years of work resulted in intellectual property being stolen along with clients and future income. Not a fun place to be in.

Legalities and parameters surrounding this were not complicated, but costs related to pursuing my losses came at a price as one would expect. Over time, these costs could have been recouped, but time invested and the distraction created could not be recovered. The day that has been given to you use wisely as it comes with God's grace. How the day is used will also reflect your relationship with God and others. After some prayer and heart-searching, I chose to disengage. My precious time would be better spent on projects that will impact my family's future, such as this book, and other things currently on the back burner, thus disengaging from the offending party. By doing so, I have cleared my mind to allocate time to opportunities that will 'progress' me and not 'hinder' me. For when you wade through a sea of untruths, you will struggle to think with clarity and one can never make sense out of nonsense. Socrates said, *"The secret of change is not to focus all your energy on fighting the old, but fighting the new."* We cannot let the tape in our head go on endless replay over old issues, for the mental energy required saps your creative thinking when preoccupied with negative events in your life. Let us review this another way. When you are so busy sorting out your *justice* in a matter of wrongdoing, you quickly forget the two most important things in your life – God and your family – in your self-righteousness, they will take a back seat. Jesus told us to turn the other cheek (*Matthew 5:38–39*) and you will only be turning the other cheek if there is a season of offence in your life. Linda (my dear wife) and I have discussed this many times, she is of the mind Jesus wants our focus to remain on him in all situations and not disclose our hand unnecessarily. Retaliation is reactionary and is based on pride; we disempower situations previously mentioned through the process of disengagement. Disengagement as an action is thoughtful, processed, being part of a strategy.

There will always be those from whom we need to disengage and you will find them in your workplaces, institutions, schools and Saturday sports. This does not require one to be unpleasant or rude or not to say hello; you simply don't engage. Not all people bring great things to the table of our lives, and we need to remain in the field of our endeavours and fruitful relationships. *"Therefore be as shrewd as snakes and as innocent as doves" (Matthew 10:16 NIV)*. Applying this also to what our eyes consume from the great LED screen in our living room or on our computers. 'Those or things' in your life, that are not uplifting to you as a person can be classified as toxic, the exact opposite of what Jesus wants for you. Life's journey is not about travelling alone; we need friends and partners to accompany us, supporting our goals and dreams.

People, who do not compete with us but complement our lives, add value like our foundation, the Lord Jesus.

One Blue Eye

> "We have all been crafted very carefully
> with a common foundation, framework
> and architecture."

ONE BLUE EYE:

You would be correct in thinking I believe Sam is perfect and I guess that is the way many people are wired about family. We look past each other's imperfections and seek to love them as they are. Strangers, when they meet Sam, are all over him and like all of us, he has an imperfection. He has one blue eye and one brown, not uncommon in his breed. Vision in Sam's blue eye is not impaired; it simply lacks pigmentation, often referred to as a walleye. Does this devalue him, not in the slightest, not in my eyes or many others, He is just a little different.

We are all different and unique; should we have one blue eye and one brown eye, be black-skinned or fair, tall or short, suffer from disabilities or dyslexia, we are individuals and masterpieces. Put us on the operating table and medical science will advise the mechanics, chemistry, neurons are the same. My broken arm or leg will be repaired the same way as a person of the same age living in a remote village in Africa and yet each one of us is still unique.

Sam's one blue eye does not hold him back; to him, it is of no consideration, yet we often allow our imperfections to hold us back. We can have one 'blue eye' on certain issues and this may require an adjustment in our thinking. Not all children fit the mould society has created in learning expectation and scholastic endeavour, and may appear to have one blue eye rather than matching eyes. In my time at college and in my senior years, I always wanted to study art. To this day, I never found out why I was denied this option, as classes were available. I was, however, streamed into the sciences, which, in turn, I replaced with music and accountancy. The outcome would be that for thirty-five years, I would work as a commercial photographer in my own business creating advertising campaigns for major brands in countries around the world. In some ways, I am like Sam, right-handed but left-eye dominant, as the viewfinder automatically went to my left eye and still does.

We have all been crafted very carefully, with a common foundation, framework and architecture. A stamp of uniqueness has been placed on every person, no matter how hard science and the world will try to pigeonhole us. Music's foundations are the same for the orchestra, jazz or rock band and those same foundations allow these different genres to share the same stage if required. Arts principalities of design, from colour and structure, are the foundations for self-expression on canvas, yet all are unique and varied, from great masters and renaissance to modernism. We have people so gifted in mathematics; that in itself is a complete language expressing the uniqueness of our universe. As diversified and gifted as we appear, our platform on this planet has only one master designer. Science has discovered the universe is constantly expanding, which is no real surprise that God is creative and does not cease. Science also recently concluded that there are more stars in the sky than there are sand grains on the shore. A fact recorded four thousand years ago when God spoke to Abraham in *Genesis 22:17,* where He compares the number of stars in the sky to the grains of sand on the beaches of the world. In *Psalm 147.4,* we are told God counts the stars, and He calls them all by name. Then, in *Genesis 1:26 NIV,* they say, *"Let us make mankind in our image, in our likeness"*. Greek and Hebrew's definition of likeness speaks about resemblance, manner and similitude. I hope this gives you an idea of truly how unique we all are.

I remember observing a safety razor blade through a microscope at school and to my surprise the cutting edge was wavy; it was not perfectly straight. Very rarely is something perfect, without flaw, without some defect or blemish. We also need to consider what the yardstick is for perfection. Day in and day out, media and institutions set their criteria for the norm and what is imperfect either by implication or by expectation. So much so, we have a world of endless competition, unattainable by any stretch of the imagination, as we may not meet these stereotyped criteria. We have all read of some beautiful young teenager with looks that would grace Vogue magazine looking in the mirror and being dissatisfied with what she sees. Sadly, her judgment is built around the media's expectation and influence of the day. Instead of seeing someone unique, she measures herself against a fictitious yardstick, losing self-confidence thus diminishing her self-esteem.

Sometimes we forget our uniqueness, focusing on our imperfections, like the girl looking in the mirror. These may be typically physical, scholastic or attitudinal traits. Generally, this occurs when we compare ourselves with others' abilities, looks and skill levels. Someone may always run faster than you, but your ability in maths will run circles around them! She may be the prettiest girl in the class, but when you sing, your inner beauty comes to the fore. Taking others' strengths and regarding them as your weakness is a falsehood and is not the attitude God expects when he has blessed you with so much. Each of us is so unique that God numbered the hairs on our head (*Matthew 10:30–32*). With such attention to detail, concern for each creation, why are we concerned about imperfections that describe each person's unique individuality?

Mass production is not part of who we are or what God desires; no set of fingerprints are the same, even our DNA is uniquely different. We are not cars, which having been manufactured on a Monday or a Friday, where the quality of workmanship could differ. Imperfections only appear by comparison. Like Sam, with his one blue eye, you may think you are a little different, this being an assumption based on a comparison. God does not see our one blue eye. He sees His creation and the purpose set aside for it. Diamonds in the rough are not really beautiful, but under the careful eye of the artisan, the facets are polished and a beautiful gem will emerge. An odd imperfection may remain, but in the eye of the beholder, it is of little concern. Jesus is without blemish or imperfection and when he looks at us it is without condemnation or judgment. He came to refine something that was already of great value and give it a life of purpose.

Within

"Personal identity needs to be founded
in something greater than the sum of our parts."

WITHIN:

Where Sam's apparent self-worth comes from is difficult to define. However, a clue may be in his loyal nature, which constantly seeks approval from me, his main carer. I see the necessities of his life are met each day and the environment in which he lives is safe. Should my voice be raised against him (very rare), his ears go down and his facial expression registers my disapproval. One pat on the head and he is happy again.

The world finds it easier to reject than accept; popularity is a whim, with external appearances holding the premier position. People who are larger physically can struggle with acceptance and often are not considered for and discriminated against in job selection. Some CEO's consider having plastic surgery to maintain a youthful appearance so career opportunities can be extended. Approval from others or peers is often the measure for their self-worth along with next accolade or achievement and recognition for awards. While these will serve to boost self-esteem temporarily, these achievements will fade and a new goal will be essential to fill the distant memory of the last one.

Foundations of self-worth are seated in our core values and attitudes, being content with knowing exactly who you are and what makes you tick. Many young people struggle with this and in today's sex-driven, drug-crazed world, my heart goes out to them. I have mentioned before that some young impressionable women measure themselves by the models on magazines who have been photographed by skilled artists with extensive knowledge of lighting, makeup and Photoshop. When they do not feel they measure up, they seek ridiculous and dangerous dieting methods. Currently, social media addiction is considered to be a bigger problem than alcohol and drugs. With little or no stigma being attached to the problem its appearance in the spotlight is limited, even though it contributes greatly to depression and anxiety.

Struggles with self-worth extend from the world's expectations of ourselves, but only if we choose to let those expectations dictate our decisions on a day-to-day basis. Consumerism is rampant, and at every level, brand management tells us what to wear, eat, drink and do. By implication, we are advised how it will make you popular; life will be much better, and you are a nicer person because of it. If you have accepted the façade offered, change this coat you are wearing (we have all worn it on occasions) and select the original coat of truth and authenticity, still hanging in the hallway; it will fit a lot better anyway.

The human spirit changes when it becomes about serving others and not one's self, when 'me' is removed from our daily vocabulary and we make choices to be intentional in our desire to help and serve others. I am a firm believer when you assist others in their ventures, the blessing you are giving will come back and this will become the mirror for yourself and your real identity. Dr Ben Carson, the famous neurologist and surgeon, said, *"We are more than flesh and bones. There is a certain spiritual nature and something of the mind that we can't measure. We can't find it. With all our sophisticated equipment, we cannot monitor it or define it, yet it is there."*

I have always enjoyed running, and I am certainly no marathon runner. It is said a marathon runner runs the first ten miles on his training, the second ten on his courage and the last six on his spirit. The first-ever marathon runner was a guy by the name of Pheidippides around 490BC and his role was that of a courier. History says he ran from Athens to Sparta for help when Persian invaders landed at the Plains of Marathon in Greece. On the first two days, he covered one hundred and fifty miles, then continued from the battlefield in Marathon back to Athens proclaiming the Greek victory against the Persians. He collapsed and died after delivering this message. Without a doubt, the lack of sustenance, hydration and heat would have caused him to succumb; however, only his spirit kept him going to deliver the message of victory. Alexander the Great wept when he surveyed his achievements, believing there were no more worlds to conquer. Can we then suppose that his self-worth was built purely on the achievements of conquering the known world? Having now consolidated these incredible goals, one of the world's most brilliant military strategists felt robbed. What had sustained his value of self-worth was now no longer available.

Having worked hard either gaining degrees or training endless hours for your place in the state sports team, the road to achieving your goals has been filled with sacrifice. However, remove these and who are you? Do not misinterpret what I am saying or consider I am diminishing the value of what you have already done. Only through hard work and commitment can you achieve anything, but your identity and self-worth, is it founded solely in these achievements? Personally, I need something more substantial than worldly expectations to be a reflection of who I am. The first verse of this scripture gives me a clue: *"Whoever dwells in the shelter of the Most High, will rest in the shadow of the Almighty" (Psalm 91:1 NIV).*

Personal identity needs to be founded in something greater than the sum of our parts and by doing this you could well become more than you think you can be. Your point of personal limitation will be removed because the yardstick is greater than who you are. If you play tennis against better players or run with faster runners, you will become better than your standard. For a business to succeed these days, it is recognised that mission statements, company ethos and the reason for the existence of a company are as important as the material returns and the balance sheet. Due to technology, the visibility of social media and trends for socially responsible companies, many shareholders want to see a company's vision is greater than just the bottom line, as it will affect the bottom line.

Self-worth has more issues today than in previous years, with the steady rise of narcissism reported, plastic surgery is at an all-time high. Attitudes supporting the theory your outward appearance will make you happier, bring fulfilment and contentment in your life and your level of acceptance will rise in the world. For us to believe any external change will benefit our self-esteem for the long term is a fallacy; it is as temporal as the smell of a new car. All long-term change has to be internal. Achievements in sport, education and work promotions are healthy, as long as our lives are not run based on fear of failure. If you haven't failed at something in life, you haven't experienced life, and should you fail, how do you deal with it? To remain fearful of failing again, you are where the world wants you. You can be down but not out, so seek the lesson that can be taken from this valuable experience, called failure, and learn from it.

This scripture *"I praise you because I am fearfully and wonderfully made" (Psalm 139:14 NIV)* says thank you, for from my God fed spirit comes courage, wisdom, strength, love, compassion, generosity of service. Your identity, when it is in Him, cannot be taken from you. The Israelites, after receiving The Ten Commandments, were given instructions to create a dwelling for God and his Covenant, as He desired to reside amongst them. An Ark of the Covenant was built and whenever this nomadic group moved, it was carried ahead of them. Through this and the New Testament, a wonderful parallel is presented to us. When we accept Christ, the Holy Spirit takes up residence within us as Jesus explains to the disciples in *John 14:26 NIV: "But the Advocate, the Holy Spirit, whom the Father will send in my name, will teach you all things and will remind you of everything I have said to you"*. As God chose to dwell in the desert, within the midst of a million of His chosen people, and over forty years went before them in every battle and challenge, so Christ does in our lives today.

Self-esteem issues are attacks on the spirit and it is not for the world to decide your self-worth as Jesus set your value with His own life. Moses had a stutter. He also killed someone in anger and became a fugitive. Samson was a sex addict, Jacob was a deceiver only to have his name changed to Israel. Rahab was a prostitute and Esther was a beauty queen who saved a nation. The list goes on. Rags and riches, addictions and exile identify these people, yet their spirit and self-worth were seated in the strength of God irrespective of their failings. Therein lay their identity.

Restoration

"Our world is an endless pursuit for
instant gratification and deadlines."

RESTORATION:

Sam is resting on the sofa surrounded by cushions, opening one eye to check all is well before he dozes off. Zeus stretches his long gangly form, climbs onto the sofa next to Sam and rolling on his back, finally settling with all fours in the air. After some minor adjustments and unusual breathing noises, both friends are asleep. As with all things that receive constant use, 'the sofa' bears hallmarks of claws and general wear and tear consistent with the occupants.

If we search in the attics of life, I am sure we would find a glorious old chair from which all lustre has gone. Cobwebs of time, dust and moisture have eroded the beautiful finish and the subtle colours of the fabric on the seat. Intricate carvings that define its personality are dulled with grime their details lost to all except the eye of the beholder. Regardless of the state and condition of this chair, its value is considerable; commanding restoration. Firstly, we need to remove all the existing varnish or polish, not an easy task; this requires both patience and dedication, hours of work and a great love for the subject at hand. Gradually, the authenticity of the chair emerges, beautiful woodgrain once lost is now apparent. Details previously indiscernible come to life all under the patient hand of the restorer.

A day arrives when the original creation is before the cabinetmaker, and the painstaking process of French polishing commences, coat after coat, layer upon layer till the wood glows with beautiful luminosity. One final step is required; he takes the threadbare seat and recovers this in a cloak of the finest silk. Once the recovered seat is returned to the chair, he steps back to study this new creation. No amount of time or cost has been spared on the chair and now the process of restoration is complete: 'He is well pleased' with his work.

Our lives are like this chair and the process of restoration begins when we visualise our 'here' and our 'there', where we are now and where we wish to be. Athletes visualise winning races and practice this as part of their mental preparation. This is no different from an artist visualising a blank canvas, a sculptor seeing form inside a piece of stone, the cabinetmaker seeing the beauty hidden in something old. Company directors have to have a vision for their companies' road ahead; the vision has to be clear and may require the removal of previous company practices and goals before their rebuilding process begins. Personal relationships can be restored when we visualise common goals, put selfishness to one side and step on to bridges with a desire to communicate.

Paring back old habits, learned behaviour, and misconceptions about ourselves are part of the journey. These attitudes will inhibit the restoration process as it would the cabinetmaker. Restoration comes with change and change also comes by stepping out of our comfort zone, visualising where we want to be, stepping on to the bridge of permission so we move forward. There is no quick fix, for it is a transformation of mind and spirit.

Paul, after his Damascus experience, spent fifteen years in self-discovery before appearing enforce on the scene. This period was the process to review all he knew, had been taught and have his value system as a brilliant academic and Pharisee turned on its head. Similarly, runners who are unfortunate enough to have suffered from shin splints due to overdoing a new training regime have to take time out to heal and be properly restored. Your training protocol will require change and how you go about further training will be under review.

Should those painful 'splints' not heal fully, they will come back to bite you. Rather like doing the same old thing the same old way and expecting a different outcome. Even Paul tells us to *"throw off everything that hinders and the sin that so easily entangles. And let us run with perseverance the race marked out for us" (Hebrews 12:1 NIV)*. To run life's race successfully, carrying a backpack full of weights is not going to get us where we wish or need to go. Permission has to be granted to the restorer to remove the old paint and varnish, and in time, others will see a new creation and the craftsmanship and patience that has gone into it.

Joseph's life *(Gensis37:2-26)* illustrates restoration's power when this seventeen year old teenager created jealousy amongst his family members due to his father's favouritism. His older brothers plotted to destroy him and instead of killing Joseph, as originally planned, they sold him to passing slave traders. As an arrogant teenager, he spent the rest of his youth and early adult years as a slave in Egypt. In time, through difficulty and many challenges, he rose through the ranks of Egyptian society and by the age of thirty, was serving the Pharaoh personally. Joseph's position was now of such power *"without your word no one will lift hand or foot in all Egypt" (Genesis 41:44 NIV).* Although severe hardship and challenges were forced on Joseph from the time he was thrown into a pit and sold into slavery, this became Joseph's point of entry in the journey of restoration. Time peeled the youthful arrogance from him and a man full of incredible wisdom, humility and integrity emerged, with a God-given gift to discern dreams which would eventually save the Egyptian nation from a terrible famine (*Genesis 41:36).*

As the famine grew in intensity *(Genesis 47:56),* many came to Egypt to augment their depleted supplies of grain from the reserves Joseph had carefully accumulated. His brothers from Canaan chose to visit for similar reasons and failed to recognise the powerful governor of Egypt as their young brother, Joseph. Twenty-three years had elapsed since they had all parted under violent circumstances. Joseph, instead of exacting revenge through his position, embraced them. Allowing for nothing to 'hinder' either his future in Egypt or the restoration of his relationship with his family. Seventy members of Joseph's family, by invitation, commenced their lives in a new land (Egypt) there by surviving the five final years of the famine. In time, this seed of the Jewish nation would grow and under the leadership of Moses and Joshua be restored to Canaan (Israel) four hundred years later.

At any stage of our lives, we can be like Joseph, stripped of his beautiful cloak and doomed to the life of a slave. We can also be the beautiful chair that Jesus wants to restore. Our world is an endless pursuit for instant gratification and deadlines, goal posts moving on us 24/7. Mankind is becoming more tarnished spiritually and lacklustre with the process of everyday living. As with the chair, we need restoration and the refuge of the cabinetmaker's workshop for the process. We restore things that are of intrinsic value and cannot be replaced, objects not found on the waste makers' shelves of the world. God, however, restores people and values and replaces righteousness, where there has been none. The cabinetmaker's work will not come to an end when the chair is complete. His work in us will never finish but requires our permission to start. As Joseph's self-righteousness had charted the initial course of his youth, God was his source and restored him and he prospered, over time, in every part of his life.

So, to whom do we go or what do we seek to restore us in times of trial and difficulty? There is no wisdom at the bottom of crystal glass or pills purchased on a dark corner; escapism is a void and its results will bear poor fruit. Joseph had knowledge and relationship with God before his journey started *(Genesis 37:5-11),* as did Nehemiah *(Nehemiah 2:18)* when Nehemiah restored the city of Jerusalem. Remarkable as these figures were in history, all had times when they ran on empty and God stepped in to restore mentally, spiritually and financially. Assisting with resources and instruction for their lives. Our first step is to ensure God's Son is welcome and established in our lives, for without access and relationship with us, how can the process of restoration begin?

The process of restoration took Joseph to new heights, transforming this young man into a skilled and humble leader, the changes being spiritual, attitudinal and physical. Any restoration commences with not only commitment but also the person not quitting. If you are addicted, marriage is rocky, business or school grades are a shambles this is not easy. Remember, when you are at the bottom, in a pit like Joseph, you can only go up, so look up and ask Jesus for help.

Bridges

"Once you step on the bridge keep moving forward."

BRIDGES:

The wind gently blows her hair as the little girl stares intently at Sam, studying his different coloured eyes. Tentatively, while her mother and I look on, she extends her hand to pat him. Her small hand gently touches and ruffles Sam's fur. In response, he licks the child's hand. Squeals of joy fill the park and Sam smiles at his newfound friend.

In a simple physical form, bridges link places that would be otherwise difficult to reach. Where a bridge would be a necessity, the lack of one either imposes on the traveller extended detours or restricts their access altogether. Common examples are either across ravines or rivers and waterways, so people and transport can communicate and access their destinations easily.

Some bridges are relational and some are metaphysical. Nations seek to create trade relations with other nations to maintain the status quo and balance of power. Trade relations create friendships and are desirable as they build trust, nation to nation, irrespective of race or creed. Relationships of this nature create understanding through the sharing of knowledge, skills and resources. Through this ongoing process of building and crossing international bridges, we diminish the risk of war. Relational bridges are not one way, as you can be standing at either end, with your destination directly ahead of you.

The film 'Bridge of Spies' directed by Steven Spielberg is a remarkable example of 'bridges' both in a physical and relational sense. Rudolf Abel, a KGB Russian spy operative, living in the USA in 1957, is captured and goes on trial in America. James B Donovan now Abel's defence lawyer, takes the case after many other lawyers refused due to its contentious nature. Mortimer W Byers, the presiding judge is urged by Donovan not to consider the death penalty due to errors in the way evidence was presented. But more importantly by enlightening him to Abel's potential usefulness, in possible future exchange programmes with Russia. Reasoning leniency in Abel's sentencing would prove prudent in the long term. Unfortunately, for Donovan, his stand and personal positioning on Abel's trial open both himself and his family to harassments and threats. While Donovan and Able are constantly making headlines, additional events are taking place. Gary Power, a US Airforce pilot, is shot down while on a routine mission, together with his U2 spy plane now falling into Russian hands. Donovan is entrusted with negotiating an exchange, Powers for Abel, together with Frederic Pryor, an innocent undergraduate student picked up by the Russians for being in the wrong place at the wrong time during the Cold War.

The first bridge crossed is the relationship between Donovan and Abel, as Donovan seeks to see justice is upheld and Abel is not subject to unfair play and biased action under US law. When the CIA asks Donovan to collaborate and disclose information that is against client/lawyer privilege Donovan refuses. Also, when the exchange between Powers and Abel is due to take place on the Glienicke Bridge, Donovan and the CIA are waiting for Pryor's simultaneous release at Checkpoint Charlie. Pryor's arrival is delayed and the CIA wants the exchange to proceed regardless, with or without Pryor. Donovan will not budge as he is prepared to cross bridges but not cross bridges with no moral grounds.

We cross bridges when we desire change; knowing where we are at the moment is no longer relevant to our lives. We seek to cross the ravine that separates us from who and where we are, to who and where we want to be. Poor relationships at home or in the workplace require someone's foot on the bridge to rebuild and create positive change. In most cases, the cost to either party is only a little humility, whereas Donovan's cost posed a serious physical risk to himself, his family and to his career. Momentum with the first step is important; once you step on to the bridge, keep moving forward, as the building process has started. Donovan kept the momentum when he would not compromise on the freedom of both Powers and Pryor, going against the tide and sentiment of the CIA.

Crossing and building bridges in your life may not always result in popularity, as it involves commitment. As I mentioned previously, you are here but need to be there. Sacrifice, as with any relationship, is the natural process of such decisions and the way many bridges are built requires people to start from both ends. How far we are prepared to go in building bridges depends on the outcome we desire. You may have to bury the ego and express humility to your staff, client, suppliers and family.

Changing your attitude from demands to one of service to others will mend bridges and build new ones. Solid bridges and only a genuine and sincere attitude of humility are required.

Relational bridges commence when a signal is given by one party to another, such as new neighbours, and is often centred around hospitality or consumption, such as a family BBQ. In business, it may be lunch or a working breakfast with your new client, a trip on someone's fishing boat or a round of golf. The bridge-building process starts with 'common ground', allowing both parties to participate in the process at their own pace. Nations send signals to the world when leaders and heads of state meet and shake hands in front of the media. Confirming visually, common ground has been established, future trade agreements are well underway and there is a mutual desire to support each other in times of crisis.

Not all signals to build bridges and establish relationships are pleasant. My signal came in 2001 when the light aircraft I was travelling in crashed after take-off. There was very little left of the aircraft, except for the cabin having remained intact. Flames were licking around the crumpled motor and five people who had to exit urgently found all the doors were jammed shut. Our pilot smashed out the front window, from which we scrambled through one at a time. None of the occupants were physically harmed, but our lives going forward would not be the same. Certain events are life changing and over the next few weeks, I recognised God was seeking my attention. My life at that time needed addressing; being built around work and business, changes were truly necessary. Years later, the experience of our aircraft falling out of the sky is still vivid, as is the realisation how badly this could have ended. Once the rescue teams arrived, and after a medical assessment, they wanted to transfer us to hospital for overnight observation. Unanimously, we decided we would prefer to move on making the three-hundred-kilometre drive home. I called Linda. "Hi, darling, how are you? I will be a little late home today as we need to drive. The plane crashed just after take-off. We are all OK."

Instead of trying to cross a deep ravine of worry and life's challenges by myself, God had given me a bridge to step on to. He was asking me to *stop* and make Him part of my life. This is not an autobiography, but I sincerely desire for you to understand how this initial step on to the bridge would carry myself and my family in future events. I hope and pray relaying this personal experience will ignite something in your life, as it did mine.

Five years later, I commenced a training programme for a long distance road cycle race. During this period of intense training however, I suddenly developed severe back pain. Over that week, pain increased to an intensity that my wife Linda had to call for an ambulance. Laced up with morphine I was rushed to a hospital. Linda and I were extremely worried that due to the amount of pain, I may have cancer in my spine. Our hospital conducted a CT scan and a ten-centimetre diameter abscess was found in my groin; this still did not explain the back pain. Ten days later, medical staff finally agreed the back pain was not in my 'head' and conducted an MRI. This disclosed a nine-millimetre abscess between L2 and L3 in my spine; the reason for the pain was now apparent. My body was sixty-three percent staphylococcal auroras infection, and intravenous antibiotics were administered twice a day for over three months in conjunction with massive painkillers to kill both infection and pain. According to doctors, should the abscess in my spine have been a millimetre larger and the infection left unchecked, I would have been paralysed or possibly worse.

It was a journey for Linda and my two children, as well as myself, and God carried us every step of the way across the bridge of healing, surrounding us with nurses, doctors and friends who helped us with each torturous step of the journey. One Christian man generously offered financial assistance; even though I knew at the time, his own business was in trouble. We declined as God had already supplied these resources; I will, however, never forget his generous offer. Friends and people kindly brought me magazines, fruit and food. Even though I could read my Bible endlessly, I could barely focus on a word in the magazines. His Word sustained and encouraged me. My spine fused naturally, strength starting to return after a year and some normality to my mobility resumed with the help of a back brace. Recollections of many of the events, time in hospital and my time at home lying flat on my back for months are hazy due to the number of drugs. What I do believe, had I not accepted the signal from our Lord to cross the bridge five years previously, the spiritual and healing strength required during this time for both myself and family may have produced a very different outcome. Scripture in Isaiah truly parallels this experience and the presence of Jesus' hand. *"When you walk through the fire, you will not be burned; the flames will not set you ablaze. For I am the LORD your God, The Holy One of Israel, your Saviour"* (Isaiah 43:2 NIV).

How far are we prepared to go when we build and cross bridges? Are we prepared to set all else aside to have great relationships with others? Two thousand years ago, Jesus was sent to the world as a bridge and mediator for humanity, an action turning this world on end, never to be the same again. He was a signal expressing God's love and desire to have a personal relationship with each one of his children (you and me), *"For there is one God and one mediator between God and mankind, the man Christ Jesus" (1 Timothy 2:5 NIV)*.

As Donovan would not leave one man behind at the Glienicke Bridge, neither will Jesus. He will wait for your first step on to the bridge and then start walking towards you, to bring you to the other side.

Endurance

> "Hardships often prepare ordinary people for an extraordinary destiny."
> *(C. S. Lewis)*

ENDURANCE:

A tennis ball flies through the air in a high lob. Sam and Zeus are off at a sprint and the game is on. Our neighbour's two dogs are barking encouragement from their side of the fence as the pair race down the hill at a breakneck pace. When the ball lands and bounces, Zeus seizes the opportunity to launch his athletic frame into the air snatching the ball from its earthbound mission. Pounding back up the hill, ball in mouth, the duo is ready to go again; endurance is a wonderful thing.

Throughout history, we see greatness thrust upon some (both man and dog!), whereas others may have scaled that pinnacle through hard work to well-earned places of achievement. Always though, any goal having been set and achieved will be replaced with another and life will set you a new target. Your skills and gifts are only a starting point for your life's foundations and direction, as the mix requires levels of endurance to carry you on the journey. Whatever the path chosen, should God be a party to the decision-making process, predetermined plans may still happen; however, now being assisted by something greater than yourself, how much more will you achieve?

Natural skills and ability are neither by chance nor by accident having both foundation and reason based within a person's spirit, your makeup. When God is involved in our choices and direction, often previously unconsidered possibilities arise in our decision-making and thinking. Due to our nature being naturally wilful, we may choose not to act on them either from personal inconvenience, fear of the unknown, or simply a desire not to step out of our comfort zone. Thinking this way can close the door to a blessing that may have been an opportunity to change our lives forever.

How we deal with important decisions and our approach to life is made very clear being instructed to *"run with perseverance the race marked out for us" (Hebrews 12:NIV).*

We all have a race to run, a life to live and are asked to do this with persistence and courage, knowing this has been marked out, predetermined and planned. Also, how and where we start this race, does not determine where we finish. Many people have commenced careers in one field and then over time, chosen completely different directions. Margaret Thatcher was originally a research chemist before going into politics. Rowen Atkinson was an undergraduate in engineering before turning to comedy and, yes, don't fall off your seat. Mick Jagger was studying accountancy. We are also instructed to run this race with perseverance and to continue steadfastly irrespective of difficulty or opposition to what we are doing. CS Lewis wrote, *"Hardships often prepare ordinary people for an extraordinary destiny",* the latter being the shaping, preparation and grooming for greater things.

Both devout Christian and remarkable athlete Eric Liddell competed in the 1924 Summer Olympics in Paris. Considerable controversy arose at the games when the 100-metre heats were held on a Sunday and Liddell would not compete in his favourite event due to his faith. Instead, he competed in the 400-metre race during the weekday, for which he received a gold medal. Liddell stated, *"I believe God made me for a purpose. But He also made me fast and when I run I feel His pleasure."* For all his natural ability bestowed upon him, Liddell had great difficulty keeping his arms still when running. They flailed the air as if fighting an invisible foe and no amount of coaching ever rectified this. Unusual as his running style was, when it was time to pass competitors on the track his head would throw back and some mighty unseen power appeared to push him to the front and across the finishing line.

To run with perseverance, we have to have stamina and endurance and this does not just happen. You have to train with purpose and deliberation, as I have found when seeking to run or cycle hills with my very limited ability. Paul says, *"Everyone who competes in the games goes into strict training" (1Corinthians 9:25 NIV),* referring to our lives spiritually as this will affect us internally and outwardly. Training teaches discipline, commitment to task and development of skill. For without, you cannot achieve the prize at the end of the race.

Endurance requires courage and stamina along with a clear vision of your goals. From this formulae purpose and deliverance result. Irrespective of the obstacles, there could well be many, it is about finishing the race and with God involved, those dreams are likely to be bigger than you. Expecting any worthy cause or venture to come at a zero cost would be foolish in the extreme, for without cost anything of true value has no value. Not entirely what we want to hear, just thinking about running or cycle training up steep hills can be exhausting! All courses marked out for us are not the same, nor will they be easy; there is, however, excellent news. We have a wonderful coach who believes in us, while knowing every step we take, he also knows our true potential.

When we have a clear picture of our goals, it is always easier to keep going as we can see light at the end of the tunnel. Should your vision appear blurry, we need to have the endurance to keep pushing through. Where we run into trouble is when reserves are depleted and we are now running on empty, not a good place to be spiritually or for life in general. With endurance, those at the back will come to the front and those at the front will remain there; without endurance, we cannot expect to succeed.

On one church wall I saw emblazoned, *"Not by might nor by power, but by my Spirit" (Zechariah 4:6 NIV),* a scripture I have thought about many times, and this verse has often had considerable influence in my life. Christian runner Eliud Kipchoge from Kenya recently ran a marathon (twenty-six miles) in 2 hours, 01 minute, 39 seconds. He says a marathon runner's success is in the heart and mind, not the legs. Many have said the marathon is a race where the first ten miles are run on your training, the second ten on your courage and the last six on your spirit. As Christians, your church and teaching received cover our training for the first ten miles. Our personal faith is the second ten, as faith requires courage, and our endurance comes from the power of the Holy Spirit in the last six miles.

Jesus will attend to the cracks and flaws in our initial training, areas of our lives that need work and like any committed coach, His job in us will never be finished. He will develop the endurance and strength required in each one of us for the conditions of every race. You may cross the finish line in a wheelchair. He will push it for you because he knows you have endured as he did. Even though life can be a marathon filled with unseen challenges and sometimes we 'hit the wall', as all runners can do in a race, remember the Holy Spirit will take us over the finishing line.

PS: Admittedly, Sam's fairly well into retirement, not quite as quick as he used to be, but the endurance is still there and so is the spirit.

A Reason for Each Season

"Seasons are different for a purpose."

A REASON FOR EACH SEASON:

Sam will not always be around to share life with myself and my family; eventually, this season will come to a close. Time and history will reveal this season as one of irreplaceable value, a time of affection, love, loyalty, companionship and new friends made from our journey together on the same road.

Nature's seasons are different for a purpose, as the ground sometimes must lie fallow before planting, so recuperation of its minerals and resources can take place. Winter frost and cold will also break up the ground in preparation for spring and new growth. Seasons of our lives show times of rejoicing, times of sadness, times of adversity of war and peace. King Solomon wrote Ecclesiastes at a time when he realised many things in his life, irrespective of his vast wealth and power, appeared futile and nothing would remain the same, the only constant being God. *"There is a time for everything, and a season for every activity under the heavens" (Ecclesiastes 3:1*

NIV), then likening man's constant futile grasping for achievements at any cost as *"and indeed, all is vanity and grasping for the wind" (Ecclesiastes 1.14 NKJV).*

Changes in our lives come through age, world events, and unforeseen circumstances, all of which are beyond our control, creating seasons in our lives of good, indifference and adversity. Should financial uncertainty or illness face you, it will affect not only you but your family and those close to you. This season, as with all seasons, will be for a time and within the framework of that window, what can we learn: patience, forbearance, trust? Seasons of adversity, no one wants, but can we shoulder the challenge, accepting the expectations of the responsibilities attached and gaining value from them? Outcomes may not always be the hopes and desires of our hearts, but what have we gained from both the journey and the season?

I met with the family surgeon to discuss the final prognosis after the onset of my father's second bout of cancer. My father had been in full remission for fourteen years, played a better game of golf than ever before (3 handicap!) and now this. I was advised that 'at this time of his life chemotherapy would be cruel and the outcome would be the same', being a qualitative life over quantity. Neither a prognosis I nor my father wanted to hear and would have to deliver to my mother and sister. Our lives moved into a new and contemplative season, knowing our beloved patriarch would not be around for his grandchildren, and the necessary burden of care to be shared during the final stages of his illness needed to be discussed. When his season closed, we had assurance he was safe and at rest with the Lord. His courage, endurance, laughter and joy under any circumstance a legacy for all his family and friends.

From seasons of grief, we gain an even greater respect for those we have grieved for and learn more about ourselves from the example that has been set for us. Our ability to deal with these seasons can leave either a positive or a poor legacy. Either inspirational or discouraging. Nothing in life is guaranteed, as I am sure you know this well, and a decision to take our hand off the outcome and our attempt to control it is not always easy. This surrender is a true step of obedience and faith when we allow Him to walk before us.

During school holidays, our family made a trip to The Remarkables ski field in Queenstown, New Zealand. My young daughter Talia asked me about the lake at the top of the mountain ski slopes. Several times in the past, I had mentioned how beautiful it was, so while we are in Queenstown, I said I would take her up there. The first time I ever made my way to the mountain top lake was in summer, and there being no snow made it a relatively easy hike. Neither Talia nor I ski (her first time to a ski field) and the only mode of transport would be a hike from the last chair lift station. Skiers and snowboard fanatics were rejoicing and celebrating very deep powder at that altitude and to my dismay, I found with each step taken I sank knee-deep in the snow! Determined not to disappoint Talia by not reaching the destination she had heard so much about, I told her to follow in my footsteps. Slogging my way to the mountain top, drenched in sweat under my thick snow jacket, an excited Talia followed gleefully behind unhindered, placing her small feet in the deep imprints I had created. Finally, we reached the lake, frozen and crystalline, against a background of needlelike pinnacles soaring steeply away from its edges. Absent of any other human presence, our efforts are rewarded with the pervading stillness and silence of this majestic scene. Some things are unforgettable because they are unique and this precious time spent between father and daughter was one of them.

I am certainly not superman, but I am a father and paving the way, as does any loving parent, for my twelve-year-old daughter made the journey not only easier for her but achievable. Our Father in Heaven will do the same for you and me, paving the way forward through his Son. Crooked paths made straight, no stone left for us to stumble on, the vipers' head crushed and the lions' roar from the thicket will be silenced. *"They will lift you up in their hands, so that you will not strike your foot against a stone. You shall tread on the lion and the cobra" (Psalm 91:12–13 NIV)*. As Talia gave me permission to lead the way, so we do need to release the control and let Jesus lead the way with the seasons in our lives and give Him the permission over the outcomes.

Disillusioned as Solomon seems with mankind and life, he finally recognises God is the only constant, appearing to have been distracted previously, but reaching a conclusion in the end that God is *"This is man's all" (Ecclesiastes 12:13NJKV)*. In either good or bad times, our response to the circumstances will or can be off-balance when we make the season the focus. Being the constant in all things, Jesus needs to be constant in all aspects of our lives: *"Jesus Christ is the same yesterday and today and forever" (Hebrews 13:8 NIV)*. In a word 'trust'. Maybe the season you are in at the moment is one of testing, as He has greater plans for you? Then realise the time of testing is the process of grooming and preparation and this is a season in itself.

My time spent with Sam on the road has been a time of contemplation, a time to listen for the voice of the Lord. This has also been a time of considerable challenge in business and direction for myself, my family, and my future. As a season, it has been one of learning and trusting God for future seasons, and the plans he has for us. Contemplating solutions my way for existing circumstances will result in *chasing the wind* in time and energy, His outcomes being in His timing, not ours and that is why we have seasons. With seasons of abundance, remember the grace and provision received that has blessed you spiritually, so you will be carried through seasons of adversity. In other words, your car runs out of gas, there is no petrol station, so start walking, should you not have a reserve tank.

We have seasons of progress and also of downturn; the latter used wisely can be used for preparation for future seasons of growth. Crops fail, droughts come, clients leave, children choose paths you do not wish for them, and jobs disappear. Nothing ever stays the same, neither with scientific opinion nor weather. Stability is vital to us all; we want this for our children our futures and our old age, irrespective there will be seasons of unrest and years of change.

Jesus' disciples went into a season of great uncertainty when they lost their Rabboni (Teacher), the cornerstone they loved had been rejected. As reprisals from the Jews were imminent, they were naturally fearful *(John 20:19)*. God's plan was in process, but neither completely apparent nor fully understood by the disciples during this time. As Solomon recognised seasons in life, *"There is a time for everything, and a season for every activity under the heavens" (Ecclesiastes 3:1 NIV),* so a time of uncertainty changed for the disciples, the unknown becoming known, declared to them and their purpose being fully established. For it is not for us to know *"times or seasons which the Father has put in His own authority" (Acts 1:7NKJV).*

Sam and I are due for a walk. It may rain, which will be good, for our winter is a dry season. Even though we may both get wet, what a blessing that will be.

Why Are You Here?

"Without God, you will never understand
why you are here."

WHY ARE YOU HERE:

Every day, Sam's life is a celebration of food, walks, games and attention from both the master and carers who surround him. Sam's very reason for being is not in question, his purpose does not contain grey areas, and although one day appears the same as the next, he is fulfilled and complete. A question of why we are here does not need validation in Sam's view, yet it still puzzles many of us.

Philosophers, universities, theological scholars, all have struggled to supply reasons to this question and the answers have been myriad. Reason, and our ability to do so, can be explained as 'judgments formed logically and are just for an action or an event'. On that basis, do we need to seek the source of this event?

Following the winter snowfall high in the mountains comes the thaw, springtime. Rivers refill and change to a bright turquoise in colour with the early melt, the minerals and freshwater irrigating the lowlands. Dry soil now refreshed and irrigated, moistens the seed and new crops commence their growth with nature's cycle being completed again for another year. For this annual occurrence, there has to be a source or fountainhead, which is the weather patterns creating the snow. Water flowing from mountains, is the source for the rivers and formation of smaller streams, similarly with mankind's work and endeavours there are tributaries and these also have a source. People working in the field of science and technology generate growth and with constant advancements in medicine and agriculture, in turn assist the sick and create food for the people on this planet. Our source for this amazing human progress commences in our minds. Man's ability to rationalise, reason, articulate, and strategically plan, places us at the head of the food chain. God reminds us of this authority: *"so that they may rule over the fish in the sea and the birds in the sky, and over the livestock and all the wild animals, and over all the creatures that move along the ground" (Genesis 1:26 NIV).* Then in verse 29, *"I give you every seed-bearing plant on the face of the whole earth and every tree that has fruit with seed in it. They will be yours for food".* We have been granted provision and resources, their utilisation and sustainability directly related to our thinking and value system. Neither we nor evolution are the source for these resources, as dominion has been attributed to us and we are therefore caretakers. God being the source.

Mankind is incredibly creative, assembling formless metal in such a way it becomes airborne, now in the shape of an aircraft, it defies the law of gravity. Our desire to paint, sculpt, build timeless structures and create music that blesses the senses and spirit are not accidents and all have a source. We do have reference to our ability to design and create. *"In the beginning God created the heavens and the earth. Now the earth was formless and empty" (Genesis 1.1 NIV).* All things created by mankind initially, have been without form and void. A classic example is the A380 airliner. Half a million kilos of metal plastic and liquid in unassembled form will remain on the ground and be of absolutely no use. However, assembled with creativity, it flies thousands of kilometres without stopping and transports people around the globe at speeds just under Mach 1. Not bad for a bunch of nuts and bolts. Creativity has a source and *"So God created mankind in His own image, in the image of God he created them;" (Genesis 1:27 NIV)*. We are surrounded by intelligent design in nature and the same skills are also embedded in us.

We debate the theories of evolution, but mankind's creativity and inventiveness has not evolved as it has always existed, it is not learned having always been with us. Only the outcome of that thinking has evolved. Pragmatically, we expand on creative thinking through experimentation, testing of ideas, trial and error and science – this is not evolution. Creativity has been in place in the minds of men from the beginning of time, linking both mind and spirit. Neurological science, however, cannot identify the mechanics or physiology for the foundation of 'mans' spirit; as the source is greater than ourselves. In *Exodus 31: 1–11,* these men were chosen specifically for their wisdom, understanding, knowledge and creative design skills to complete work for the tabernacle. When the massive civil engineering project of restoring the city of Jerusalem arose, it was passed to Nehemiah, a man with vision, creative ability, and organisational skills. Nehemiah was also not short of friends in high places, having financial support and assistance granted from King Artaxerxes for the rebuild. However, for the success of the project, Nehemiah placed personal reliance on God as we see in this scripture *"I also told them about the gracious hand of my God on me" (Nehemiah 2:18 NIV)*.

As weather sources at high altitude are transformed with each new season, the benefits become apparent in the land below. New life and growth are being brought about and annual cycles are completed once again. Not that different from our lives, as we must feed and nourish not only our bodies but mind and spirit as well. Good nutrition feeds our muscles and organs, giving them the strength to go the distance. Our mind also needs to be renewed in its method of processing, assessing and digesting life and all that is entrusted to us. Just as we are required to eat to live, otherwise starve to death, you have to renew and refresh your mind by going to the source for the correct nourishment.

History is littered with giants and legends whose unsurpassed achievements never cease to amaze the world and yet some were left questioning the point of their own existence. Many of those finding no answer have despaired at this conclusion, as their worth was centred around their abilities, not recognising the true source for them.

In the aftermath of single-handedly defeating four hundred and fifty prophets of Baal and redeeming the relationship between God and the Israelites, Elijah fled. Jezebel, the reigning queen at the time, on learning of Elijah's victory, threatened to find and destroy him *(1Kings19:1-2NIV)*. Hiding in a cave almost suicidal with depression, God asked Elijah to come to the mouth of the cave so He could reveal Himself *(1 Kings19:11NIV)*. Elijah's expectation of the situation may have been that God would show up in person and yet the scene at the cave entrance was vastly different. Winds so powerful that rocks and mountains moved, a terrible fire, and lastly an earthquake.

God's power was truly evident, but where was God?

In the subsequent silence, a small clear voice spoke to him. *"What are you doing here, Elijah?" (1 Kings19:13NIV)*

We all can be faced with 'what are you doing here' or 'why am I here', as questions they are similar. Elijah's physical and mental location of both isolation and despair had a reason – an event. With new direction and instructions, God helped him understand his existence and purpose, showing Elijah a way forward. Although in a cave physically, his mind was also in-shrined by the darkened surrounds. Without God, you will never fully grasp why you are here and I am sure you agree the 'whys' in life need answers. As with all things, we are the result of an event and every event has a source. Your search for the source, excluding God the Creator, will bring you to a point where every event reaches a void, there is an abyss: *as was the earth when God's Spirit, the source of all we are, hovered over its surface.*

An Eagle's Perspective

"In the language of imagery, perspective is a point of view."

AN EAGLE'S PERSPECTIVE:

Resting on the hillside, Sam and I observed two eagles soaring effortlessly on invisible air currents and thermals. Their fluid grace contrasting sharply with our weary state, due to our long hike and the warmth of the late afternoon. Apparently tireless in their activity, these beautiful creatures continued to perform amazing aerodynamic skills, only to eventually depart. After being privileged to such an air show, they, in time, became specks in the sky, so we gathered ourselves up and moved on.

An eagle's provision is derived from their ability to detect wind currents (science has no finite answer as to how) and with a simple launch becoming air-born with limited effort. In turn, we labour valiantly in the provision process to meet our families' needs. We, however, should recognise how God has blessed these majestic predators of the air to rely not on their own strength, but God's provision of thermals and air currents for their survival.

Family, news, work and business surround us every day and cannot help but colour our thoughts, acting as filters of information for daily life. Due to these filters, our perspective on how we see things may not always be correct. In the language of imagery, perspective is a 'point of view'. When you move a camera around a subject, something will increase in size and others will diminish, or vice versa. With this in mind, consideration should be given to how we view our circumstances: is our cup half full or is it half empty? When we observe or are shown things from different perspectives, attitudes, emotional states and relationships can change.

I believe most people struggle with difficult situations, finances and health, possibly family, we naturally become physically, emotionally and spiritually tired. Invariably, our perspective will become negative, searching for answers from worldly sources where-as looking from God's viewpoint this may require matters to be handled differently. We need to surrender all things to Him. My father was neither short on wit nor wisdom and very often I heard the expression, 'they can't see the wood from the trees', referring to situations where we are so close to, we cannot see the obvious and our ability to consider another viewpoint or perspective is limited. Handing over control to gain a new perspective, revelation and understanding of what God wants is far from easy, since the human race has been granted free will from the dawn of mankind. However, as eagles launch from a nest high in the mountains, trusting in the provision of the thermals to support their mighty bodies in flight, we also need to surrender and launch in faith as they do.

The following scripture explains the grace and provision already in place for us, *"but those who hope in the LORD will renew their strength. They will soar on wings like eagles; they will run and not grow weary, they will walk and not be faint." (Isaiah 40.31NIV).* His provision is already present as for these mighty birds of the air, we only need to seek God's perspective on how he views our circumstances. Many times, we wear ourselves out seeking solutions to situations that appear unresolvable when all we are required to do is launch in God's strength. Our compatriot, high on his rocky ledge, must hunt to survive and launches without hesitation trusting for provision to support his task ahead, so must we. Our perspective or viewpoint of all things is encapsulated when Jesus taught his disciples to pray, *"Let it be done on earth as it is done in heaven."* We are being instructed to see things from His perspective and to act according to His ways. David did not view Goliath from the same perspective as the Israelite army, if he had, this remarkable historic standoff would never have happened. David's faith allowed him to view the giant as God viewed him, prideful and vulnerable as any mortal man.

So, why do we fail to launch?

Fear of the unknown? Yet we have faith – hope in things unseen and yet to come? Or do we let the power of the world be so woven into the fabric of our lives that our perspective remains at ground zero? The change of viewpoint is not by accident, not by default, but by choice. One of the most glorious things in life is to place your children on your shoulders showing them the world from your viewpoint, for when they are little, their perspective is vastly different from ours. Scriptures give us His advice on every circumstance in life and by reading them, the opportunity is granted to stand shoulder to shoulder with the Lord and see what He sees. Both

Old and New Testaments show us the frailty of man, his triumphs and failures, the reasons for both. Our world will never take time to sit down and tell you why you screwed up, but God will as we see with Nathan confronting David over his sin with Bathsheba *(2 Samuel 12)*. Mostly it will remain in the too hard basket with any restitution and personal change only being a distant possibility.

Questions concerning the Bible's relevance today have been raised, yet what is the difference between adultery, greed, murder, theft, envy and pride in the twenty-first century and 5,000 years ago? None. Broken marriages are broken for the same reasons, wars are fought and genocide is committed or planned for the same reasons, children leave the nest, spreading their wings and some soar and some crash and burn. Reasons for these situations are still the same and so are the solutions. You can attach some clever buzzwords to them repackaging the answer, but the foundation to both circumstance and solution has already been well scripted.

His thoughts and ways are not our ways and who is to know the mind of God! However, His written word explains His requirements for our thoughts and actions for life's journey. This perspective is vastly different from the foundations of learning in government institutions today. Some universities in the US are now considering teaching wisdom. Whose wisdom will be taught? In the beginning, the world was formless and the Spirit of God hovered over the waters; wisdom existed because God existed. Any first step to wisdom is the knowledge of God, so let us not put the cart before the horse. Wisdom will change our perspective, give us many viewpoints, understanding in all matters, unbiased decisions, compassion and sound judgment. All of this comes with the knowledge and acceptance of God and sounds very much like Jesus our Lord.

Currently, this book represents one of several projects I am working on. The others being financial priorities and workflow, each day commencing with work on business projects and getting around to 'the book' as time permits. Expectations of my business projects were not meeting desired levels and if anything, seemed more and more challenging. During an afternoon walk with Sam, I asked the Lord for help on this matter and writing this book was made clear by our Lord as the first priority of each day. Changing my workflow immediately, I saw changes within two weeks. My perspective and approach moved from what I considered important to what He wished to be my priority. Maybe I am a slow learner and just as your cup is half full or half empty, we need to give our Lord a chance to work on the half-full part and let it overflow.

Due to our free will, many consider scripture a list of don'ts, a perspective of inconvenience, a worldly view rather than seeking an eagle's perspective, God's view. For a plan of life to be laid out before you in a tapestry of aspirations and potential achievements, we need to understand, *"What no eye has seen, what no ear has heard, and what no human mind has conceived the things God has prepared for those who love him". (1Corinthians2:9–10 NIV)*. Having read this far, you most likely have a relationship with our Lord, and I pray that will go from strength to strength. Should you not know God, set aside time to ask Him into your life, and start seeing things from His perspective.

You will be amazed at how He will refresh your outlook, *you shall run and not grow weary and you shall walk and not grow faint.*

The Thin Blue Line

"For a constant to exist, it has to be ceaseless,
loyal, unfailing, permanent and infinite."

THE THIN BLUE LINE:

Something Sam has not seen is the 'thin blue line' separating living things on earth from outer space. Space flight has allowed mankind to observe this phenomenon and I ask you to grant me some artistic licence to call this the 'line of life'. From Sam's point of view, the reason for the ball falling from the sky and landing is irrelevant; all that matters to Sam is it's fun. He could not care about gravitational pull or the troposphere and yet this veil of protection that encircles the earth is what sustains both him and me.

For us, the thin blue line is the very reason you and I can breathe, similarly with all other creatures on this earth over which man has been given dominion. Existing knowledge of the solar system shows we are unique, and via complex space telescopes we are witness to multiple universes and other planets. It appears we are unique to have a 'thin blue line' placing earth in a protective cocoon. My conclusion is that we are seeing the uniqueness of our God who understands our needs, a God who created us in his image. How else can you explain the solitary blue planet and its thin blue line, supporting life, in an ever-expanding universe? Ongoing research by the finest brains in science and physics has completed complex mathematical formulae seeking explanations but never places a power greater than man in their equations. For the very existence of our universe, there does need to be a reason. I do not believe it was just an accident and although the miraculous hand of creation is also difficult to comprehend and truly challenges the mind, to me this is the most acceptable answer we have.

Man's quest for answers from the cosmos, from the time of the Babylonians and Egyptians who were the forerunners and basis of Greek astronomy, has been never-ending. We now realise in our twenty-first century that our universe is constantly evolving. As God's work continues in the ever-growing universe in the inhabitable atmosphere beyond the thin blue line, so does His work in you and me. Will this work ever cease? I know the work that God does in each person on earth, when given permission, will not be complete until we leave and take a place of permanent rest with Him. As people and nations refuse to listen to Him, a time will arrive when the burden of discarded responsibilities will come home to rest globally for mankind. To many, it must be obvious that people and the path the world is on cannot be sustained. Convenience and speed of air travel have placed greater risk for pandemics, with many current antibiotics now completely ineffective due to new strains of superbugs. Millions still continue to starve and die from prevalent famines and disease; governments are forced to spend billions on arms races to maintain power and secure borders against countries with irresponsible leadership that support terrorism.

The protective bubble of the thin blue line, about ten kilometres deep, is all that separates us from existence and extinction and 'Grace' is a word that comes to mind when I consider this miracle given to all the world. Our extremely fragile circumstance so carefully encapsulated at the time of creation, contains the same principalities and world eco-structure that sustained Abraham and his family four thousand years ago, as it does today for you, me and Sam.

God's foundations for mankind have not changed, however, man has developed a contrary methodology. Because we apparently know better!

Family and government leadership from history parallels today with all the same challenges, only compounded by the speed of communication and technology – yes, there is a downside to our advances. Our relational skills of personal interaction are being eroded and social media has given advent to cyberbullies whose courage is limited to pressing buttons on their touch-tone phones. Yet, the principles of the issues that seek to confound do not differ from the human race at the beginning of time. All the while, the thin blue line still remains constant, sustaining and supporting new life, yet little consideration is given to the One who created this.

We all have many unanswered and detailed questions regarding life in this ever-changing world and as the thin blue line is a constant for our very existence, so is God constant in every way. In *Malachi 3:6 NIV*, *"I the LORD do not change. So you, the descendants of Jacob, are not destroyed"*. This is not limited to Judaism and the Old Testament. In *Galatians*

3:8NIV, we are reminded God spoke to Abraham, *"All nations will be blessed through you"*.

The change will never cease, as God is creative and the universe surrounding us keeps evolving and as mankind is made in 'His image', we naturally want to create, advance ourselves and invent. However, if man and what he does are constantly changing but have no constant, we have no real foundation to build on. When you renovate your home interior the foundations remain the same, in mathematics there are constants for probability formulae enabling the variables to arrive at an appropriate answer. We also, need a constant in our lives. Neither is your career a constant nor your finances, health or college degrees; they are resources and the constant to all these is a source. In *Hebrews 2:5 NIV*, *"What is mankind that you are mindful of them, a son of man that you take care of him?"* He is mindful of us because He cares and loves His creation and wishes to bless us with many good things. Because of this we also need to be mindful of Him.

For a constant to exist, it has to be ceaseless, loyal, unfailing, permanent and infinite. Unfortunately, these characteristics are not typical or represent the ways of our world. People are left to struggle with the governmental inconsistencies and ever-changing requirements of society and its expectations. When we are in our Father's house, we have a constant *"Surely goodness and love will follow me all the days of my life, and I will dwell in the house of the Lord forever" (Psalm 23:6 NIV)*.

Looking out the window at the blue of late afternoon sky, the shadings make the heavens appear hemispherical and easy to envisage the thin blue line encompassing us. Our atmospheric divide between life and eternity, gravity and weightlessness placed carefully for our protection so God can enjoy you and me, His creation. How this all happened it is hard to know. Theories can get tiresome; they are so often inconclusive. Still, from the dawn of creation, it was planned by God, who was fully mindful of conditions needed to sustain those he would create in His image.

Being a beautiful spring evening, it's a bit late for a walk. I will give Sam and Zeus a game instead.

Your Seed Your Legacy

"Understanding and accepting failure in life is a necessary process to equip us for the next step forward."

YOUR SEED, YOUR LEGACY:

Man's relationship with canines has puzzled scientists for years, with research indicating we have a closer relationship with them than primates. Why our four-legged friends show such affection for us and vice versa is certainly a paradox and at the moment there are no hard and fast answers. Sam, as an example, projects sacrificial giving, unconditional love for his family and respect for his master. Endless stories are recorded about dogs, in all shapes and sizes, coming to the rescue of their masters, protecting children and servicemen, placing our lives before their own. Closer to home, my father, as a young man, was caught in an undertow while swimming. Calling to his red setter Molly playing in the shallows, she swam out to him and towed him safely to shore through the surf.

We have some clues when we see a dog's ability to have an understanding of right and wrong – more so than any other creature it appears in the animal kingdom. An ability believed to stem from their wild heritage – the wolf. Where a disciplined family system is in place, selfishness and greed are unacceptable to the pack ethos and loyalty to the pack being above all. I can say with confidence that Sam is derived from good seed, and the by-product of this is a great legacy to all those around him and who are in contact with him.

We all need to be sowers of good seed in the foundations of our society, family and companies. Although this may appear obvious, it does not appear to be the case in modern man's progress, as we continue to fail and send the ambulance to the bottom of the cliff to falsely achieve a better outcome. For humans to endeavour to expect results that reflect values of integrity, loyalty, unconditional love, and wisdom, the planters and sowers must cast good seed. I am sure you agree that this makes good sense. This seed must be the very essence of who we are (like Sam and his heritage) and be seated in the foundation of our Creator, God. Possibly, we could conclude, for those who question Gods existence, suggesting we are only a group of evolved cells, then any seed of intrinsic value is immaterial.

Irrespective of what we teach, the who and the why will be prevalent in young people's minds and the sowers need to afford each generation the opportunity of this knowledge. For the sake of political correctness, administrators in both government, education systems and universities continue to deny future generations the value and importance of God's existence. Why? It's an inconvenient truth. Darwinism and the science of evolution are taught, yet proof of fossils representing the change from the simplest or most primitive life form to the complex man have never been found.

Outcomes of the current pattern of removing biblical understanding and teaching in schools deny young people the opportunity of wise life choices. As some subjects at school are compulsory, should not the basic principles of living also be taught? Western-based nations continually diminish true foundational values for young adults through current education curriculums. These decisions, manifesting later in young people as a lack of self-worth, drug addiction, teen suicide and many other issues we have in society. As our desire for sowing good seed diminishes from generation to generation, a crumbling moral legacy is left for society to patch up.

Science serves agriculture well by changing the DNA of seed structure to perform well under specific climate and or adverse conditions. We train young minds to think and advance their skills to achieve and succeed, yet we lower the bar when we come to sowing seed of moral fibre, compassion, integrity and selflessness. The DNA required for anyone of us to flourish irrespective of circumstances and conditions. Therefore, any expectation for a legacy of better values in future generations is decidedly naive on our part, as what we can be and the goals we strive to attain, are founded in endlessly compromised convictions.

Sowing starts at the top; the head of the family, the CEO and good seed will filter down and be watered. As one parent sows, one must water and endorse the other (no head of the household debates please!). Company directors sow to their appointed executives equipping them to water and endorse their vision down the chain, and with correct values, imparted and learned in such a way they will not be forgotten – you now have a legacy.

Any sower casting seed is seeking to prosper from his work, which is why he casts the seed! As sower, he also needs to prosper those around him and therefore must cast evenly with diligence on his fields. Ensuring seed is of good quality, the ground is fertile, and well prepared. All relationships, business and personal, require we check the ground of the field carefully before investing time and energy, then we can be confident it will produce good fruit. Sometimes those who water the sown seed are not present at the time of sowing, but they will come, it will be watered – endorsed – and there will be a good harvest.

There is only one source of good seed: the living God. Yet we choose to either ignore or remove from our society all which He wishes to sow in us: *"Every good and perfect gift is from above, coming down from the Father of heavenly lights, who does not change like shifting shadows". (James 1:17 NIV).*

Mistakes are the foundation of all learning (I have made plenty), and in business, if the mistake is pointed out you are blessed for so often the mistake you have made is not apparent. Understanding and accepting failure in life is a necessary process to equip us for the next step forward. None of us desire the disappointment that comes after hours or years of hard work, with results not meeting expectations and outcomes. Whether this occurs in your sport, academic or work pursuits, young people's tolerance for failure today has diminished, they are struggling. Let us be responsible and show them disappointment is a great teacher and has a positive spinoff and when embraced you will be stronger for it. *"But he said to me, My grace is sufficient for you, for my power is made perfect in weakness" (2 Corinthians 12:9 NIV).*

Sow the seeds of resilience and persistence in your children and your companies. Teaching values of integrity, courage, honesty and loyalty, a legacy that will carry them and your staff into the future. In certain nations where title and position are more valuable than the learning, students can 'purchase' their degrees, devaluing both degree and person. Poor seed distributed to young minds by status-driven parents who place so much value on title and position, any value of character building is dismissed. For as John W Gardner wrote, *"The society which scorns excellence in plumbing as a humble activity and tolerates shoddiness in philosophy – neither its pipes nor theories will hold water."*

A vision shared is seed sown. Jesus illustrated clearly how to lead by example, through the action of washing the disciples' feet. In antiquity, when groups gathered at a person's home to share a meal, they reclined on the floor, resting on cushions. Their feet now revealing exposure to the dirty and dusty roads they had recently travelled. Out of courtesy it was necessary for a person to be hired to wash the guests' feet, a job considered by many a lowly task. In *John 13:14–17NIV,* Christ demonstrates His humility and servanthood to his disciples: *"Now that I, your Lord and Teacher, have washed your feet, you also should wash one another's feet. I have set you an example that you should do as I have done to you".*

This famous event paints a powerful image where Jesus' counter-cultural actions added value and lasting legacy to his team, and those who would come to know Him. His expectations of servanthood, humility and the message He wanted to be delivered to the world being expressed in a single action. Rebuking the disciple's prideful discussion during the Last Supper *(Luke 22:24)* and from a position of authority, His own humility displayed his vision for them. In today's language, He swept the workshop floor, although being above all. *"As surely as I live, says the Lord, every knee will bow before me; every tongue will acknowledge God" (Romans 14:11 NIV).*

A mighty seed was sown in the upper room that day falling on fertile ground, a legacy set in place for thousands of years to come. Great artists such as Leonardo da Vinci were inspired by Jesus actions to envisage and paint the 'Last Supper' and Tintoretto's masterpiece depicting Jesus washing his followers' feet.

Even though we are blessed with the artists' vision and genius of this historical event, it is the seed in our minds and hearts that change attitudes, becoming the moral compass for ourselves and our children and our children's, children.

One more thought, Peter said to Jesus, *"You shall never wash my feet."*

Jesus answered, "Unless I wash you, you have no part of me." (John 13:8 NIV).

Have you let God wash your feet?

Who Is the Master?

> "We need to master ourselves more than
> skills and gifts for a great life, and that
> can only happen when we appoint the master, Jesus."

WHO IS THE MASTER:

There is little variation, day to day, in Sam's life. Exciting new events, additions to his daily activities change little, as the majority of each day's routine is entrusted to me, his master. Just the other day he was looking stiff and tired and with a longer than normal walk planned I decided against taking him. When I returned from my walk, he would barely make eye contact with me. I certainly was not his favourite person till after the evening meal when he chose to rest at my feet by the couch.

Our mindset is such when we plan a project we have an assumed outcome and expectation. When results do not reflect our initial expectations, we may see our endeavours turn to forcing the outcome and more often than not it still does not work out. Letting go of things once planned and accepting the outcomes is a challenge for all of us, when we are disappointed and frustrated with results falling short of our original desires; possibly blaming others – a bit like Sam.

Planning for work, exams, trip overseas, a holiday, we open a door to fresh possibilities and walk through with a view of something better on the other side. Should the 'something better' not happen (the best-laid plans of mice and men), our attitude of acceptance determines our ongoing approach and steps. Many athletes and sportsmen have positive training performance, but when they hit the competition, they don't make the podium. Very often, their focus is centred on the outcome. It is easy for their focus to shift from the journey, or task at hand, to the final outcome. Any personal desire to win is not minimised, and that should not be presupposed. Simply, the energy focus moves from the game to the goal. When we give one hundred percent to playing a shot in golf or tennis, scores on the board generally start to take care of themselves. One substandard delivery in the game may not always be the beginning of a sinking ship, and the correct focus will cultivate an attitude necessary to be a game changer. Many situations require our release of an outcome, and a rechannelling of our focus is the key, with the sum of the parts becoming the whole. Think of it this way: your watch is constructed of intricate parts each made with great skill; therefore, your expectation is for the mechanics to function correctly and tell the time accurately.

David walked through the door of faith. *"Let no one lose heart on account of this Philistine; your servant will go and fight him" (1 Samuel 17:32 NIV),* confident of the outcome in a one-on-one with Goliath. Jonathan, the son of King Saul, and his young armour-bearer, took the fight to the Philistine camp unaided. *"Come, let's go over to the outpost of those uncircumcised men. Perhaps the LORD will act in our behalf. Nothing can hinder the LORD from saving, whether by many or by few" (1 Samuel:14:6 NIV).*

Any of these scenarios, had they gone wrong, posed deadly consequences for the initiators, yet in both cases each goal and mission was successful. If David had focused on or had any adverse thoughts about the outcome, he may have missed with his slingshot. Should Jonathan have considered that both he and his armour bearer were greatly outnumbered (which they were), they may have failed.

In a recently televised series about the astronaut selection process, the final three (very excited and remarkable men and woman) contestants were given some very sobering and important truths. The chance of death by misadventure in space exploration is 35%. Your chances of dying in a car crash 1:303 (0.33%) and soldiers serving in Desert Storm 1:3162 (0.316%). All far better odds than attempting a space mission, regardless, the candidates accepted the possible risks and continued with the programme.

Unlike these men from the pages of history, David, Jonathan and the young armour-bearer, not all people have God as part of their lives to approach dangerous challenges with this apparent lack of concern for their welfare. Certainly, as men, there would have been inner emotions about the situations they chose to face; nevertheless, they mastered emotions of doubt and fear through God's grace and strength. We all pass through doors every day, some good, others not so pleasant, sometimes we have a family member or friend with us for support, sometimes we don't – as this cannot always be guaranteed. Doors we go through can open unexpectedly or be a choice, and Jesus, as with David and Jonathan, has no desire for you to do this journey by yourself.

Someone has to be the master and most guys would like to think they are the masters of their own destinies – it's a 'bloke' thing! Consideration and thought needs to be given to the word master. By English definition, someone who is in complete control of something, a master of classical piano, painting, business administration, a classroom. In Greek, the word is 'despotes', meaning absolute power and in Hebrew and Aramaic 'Rabboni', a title inferred only on the head of the Sanhedrin (Jewish religious sect) for a whole nation.

We may be master of our skills and gifts, but have we mastered ourselves? Considering also when we apply the previously mentioned language derivations, this means total and absolute control of all things. Do we control each day and the difficulties that come through the door? Your promotion, is this guaranteed? Are the health, safety and future of your children and family assured? You may say we have governments for regulations and systems in society to reduce risk, so why then do we have lawyers and insurance companies? Prevention is definitely better than cure but does not always cure.

Sporting competitors during games throw racquets on the ground in frustration and anger or seek to gain a positive advantage by manipulating circumstances or their equipment. Manipulation of documents by mortgage lenders to push loans through before the GFC is little different from a student cheating in exams. Actions such as these show how little we master ourselves and our inability to cope with the outcomes we desire to control. We need to master ourselves more than skills and gifts for a great life, and that can only come when we appoint the ultimate master and leader, Jesus. One challenge (of many) that arose when I chose Christ was mastering my tongue. Many major companies have overseas call centres to assist with IT issues, dial the number and you will go through a crazy number of hoops to get an answer. Half an hour later, still listening to elevator music, my fuse has been lit as I am now apparently being 'escalated in the system!' After supplying no remedy to my many requests, it is suggested a call back needs to be arranged for the next day. Unfortunately, my response would be blunt and curt, this is not what Jesus wants. For when we tame the tongue, we truly master ourselves, as explained in detail in *James 3:1-18NIV* and having read this many times, I pray I have finally got there.

We have to let Jesus Christ be the master of our outcomes and motivated self-achievers can find that quite a challenge with the word 'self' being the problem. Replace the word self with 'God', and we will view outcomes from His perspective and not the worlds. David, as a shepherd boy, was an achiever and extremely self-sufficient, alone at night with the threat and danger of wild animals during a time of total lawlessness. His skill with the sling was not the means by which he toppled a giant clad in armour; it was David's faith in God enabling him to surrender the outcome. All David's preparation and decisions before his engagement with Goliath were based on previously, proven and tested parameters as a shepherd: *"David fastened on his sword over the tunic and tried walking around, because he was not used to them.*

I cannot go in these, he said to Saul, because I am not used to them" (1 Samuel 17:39 NIV). David's statement refers to the weight and unfamiliarity of both sword and armour. As a shepherd boy his faith had already been tested in God, whom he trusted over any resource made available by men.

Preparation is a wonderful and essential tool. David went through this process knowing for the next thirty minutes or more his faith would be his cornerstone and shield. Ultimately you are never fully in control as there will always be things beyond your control. Fast-changing world events continue to impact and rapid development of artificial intelligence and robotics will remove more personal control from mankind. Under whose control and auspices will yours and your family's life depend; databased computers of the future making life's important decisions? Think about this? We all have some master or masters and our lives will be a reflection of who they are. Jesus Christ, the Son of God who cares for me and my family, is my master. He helps with the tasks large and small and His wise counsel helps you master yourself.

Jesus was in the stern, sleeping on a cushion. The disciples woke him and said to him.

"Teacher, don't you care if we drown?"

He got up, rebuked the wind and said to the waves, "Quiet! Be still!"

Then the wind died down and it was completely calm.
(Mark 4:38–39 NIV)

He who calms the sea is my master, who is yours?

On a Hill Far Away

"Climbing is always intentional
at the very least."

ON A HILL FAR AWAY

Zeus races back up the hill after retrieving the ball. Sam follows close on his heels, pushing hard to keep up with him. Even with legs a little shorter than the lanky pointer, Sam will expend all his energy to keep up. Sounds of lapping tongues at the water bowl followed by breathless panting precedes the duo's final collapse on the veranda furniture, where they regain their strength for yet, another game.

Many dangerous and difficult mountains have been climbed and conquered by brave and skilled mountaineers, Everest by Sir Edmund Hillary, the Matterhorn by Edward Whymper, and without doubt there are many others. Mountains in life come in all shapes and sizes, in a way each to his own; what is not a mountain for one person being the nemesis for another. We always have three choices: stay at the bottom, climb for a while and quit, or make sure we get to the top. There is a table prepared for those who reach the summit. They will be rewarded with the beauty of the view, a landscape of opportunities laid before them and an ability to see storms that hover on the horizon.

When we modify our thinking and become intentional in our attitudes and approach, we also transform our spirit. Every climb will have a price and the cost will only come through effort and change. You will not get fit for a marathon sitting on the sofa munching crisps, drinking sodas and watching soaps. When we decide to climb and make those first steps, we do so intentionally, to reach the top – not just hoping. If we only hope to make it, we do not climb in faith; when we climb in faith, we climb with intention and courage – assurance.

After the passing of Moses, Joshua was entrusted with moving over a million people to their inheritance, a new land and thereby fulfilling God's promise to his people: *"Now then, you and all these people, get ready to cross the Jordan River into the land I am about to give to them – to the Israelites" (Joshua 1:2 NIV).* Although well trained by his mentor Moses, Joshua was aware of the oversized shoes he had to fill and the challenges to his abilities and skills that would be placed on his new office of leadership. Any person however well trained, would have doubts and apprehension's concerning their abilities for Joshua's mammoth task. Being all knowing the Lord was aware of this. Joshua was told not once but three times he was to *"Be strong and courageous" (Joshua 1: verses 6:7:9 NIV).* Clear instruction to have courage, take ownership, irrespective of his personal doubts or fears as these would not suddenly vanish. However, *"Keep this Book of the Law always on your lips; meditate on it day and night, so that you may be careful to do everything in writing in it" (Joshua 1:8 NIV)*. I (God) will be present and you can do this.

The shapes and sizes of mountains differ, as do challenges and the people that choose to accept them. Examples of those who have climbed in God's name are present in the Hall of Faith *(Hebrews 11)*, some descended into dark places through weakness, rising again to the top. Prophets and prostitutes made great in their failings, but in the name of God, imperfect as they were, they placed one foot after the other and chose to climb.

On a televised interview conducted by Canon J Johns, Lord Michael Hastings (Global Head of Citizenship for KPMG International) shared how cynicism was one of the largest issues and stumbling blocks to overcome when it came to companies supporting his projects. Cynicism he said produces apathy and how often have we heard a problem is so great, what difference could we possibly make? Mother Theresa when asked about the impact she was having with her work replied *"We, ourselves, feel that what we are doing is just a drop in the ocean but the ocean would be less for that drop."* Apathy will always keep us at the bottom of the mountain, the personal change will never come from 'it's too late now' or 'I could never do that' and 'we don't have the resources'. Apathy will keep you on the sofa with the soaps, crisps and sodas.

Climbing is always intentional; at the very least, you are choosing to go against the grain, against gravity. As you head up a steep hill in your car, you have to change down a gear. If you are running, you shorten your stride (I have to). Intentionality comes from attitude change, looking at possibilities and seeing your failures, mistakes and near-disasters as valuable lessons not to be repeated. When you intentionally commit to the climb, expect possibilities also from unexpected and sometimes very different quarters. Even though you had specific reasons for initiating the climb, you may surprise both yourself and others at the outcome when you reach the top.

It is one thing to be satisfied and pleased with the result at the top of any hill; however, did you succeed on the way up as well? Was every challenge barely coped with along the way, or did you choose to embrace the opportunities that tested you? Understanding the journey was as important as the arrival, this took me a while to grasp. Road cyclists know that hills are the real deal. You train on the hills and race on the flats. Your disliking hills is not an option as it's part of the package and skill as a cyclist. Lance Armstrong made a remarkable come back from cancer and through a gruelling training regime, he had to repeat hill climbs again and again until they were completed in the required time. This is where attitude and intentionality gain altitude.

Necessity may be the mother of invention, but vision and purpose will partner with you when you choose to climb the mountain in front of you. After being in slavery for four hundred years, you and I would be like the Israelites lacking vision and purpose and the idea of moving to the unknown would be daunting. Mountains and hills they had to climb had names; they were called doubt, fear, procrastination, ungratefulness and rebellion. Regardless of the miracles that surrounded them day and night (*Exodus 13:21–22*), they could not see the big picture and remained at the base of those mountains for forty years, when their journey should have only taken eleven days. Intentionality comes into play when we decide on the eleven-day journey and not the forty-year version, leaving no room for apathy.

Two mountains changed the course of world history aeons ago and their impact still resonates with us today. Three thousand four hundred years ago, Moses climbed Mt Sinai and received the Ten Commandments, simple guidelines and the foundation by which God asked his people, then and now, to conduct our lives. Although given to us in commandment form, it has been done with love and care for 'all' people of this world. God's goal is to protect us and our families, to instruct us with wisdom and life skills, sound decision making, so things will go well in our lives: *"what is mankind that you are mindful of them, human beings that you care for them" (Psalm 8:4 NIV).* Writings from the psalmist resonated fourteen hundred years later when Jesus climbed Golgotha outside the city wall of Jerusalem, already half dead from loss of blood and scourging, to be crucified.

Through His sacrifice and through him only *(John 3:16),* every man, woman and child, has access to God's Kingdom. The hill outside the city wall, that Christ climbed, was a mountain, a place of unimaginable suffering and sacrifice and on that day cynicism and apathy were not present.

Instead, vision, purpose and sacrifice, the ingredients for anything of true value were present in their purest form, keys to all great mountain climbing.

Sam's Paintbox

"As each person's canvas is created,
the colours change with their circumstances."

SAM'S PAINTBOX:

When Sam came into the world, his life was a blank canvas; our family's existence or where life's adventures and events would take him, were a big unknown. Circumstances surrounding Sam's origins and previous ownership are sketchy, as he was supposedly eighteen months old when he joined our family. With the hard work of the farm, now behind him, his point of view registered the benefits of graduating to city dweller and the run of our house. Add to this overseas travel, with our shift from New Zealand to Australia. Sam's circumstances have changed dramatically over a few years and so have the colours on the canvas of his life.

All of us start with a blank canvas. I often look at children, wondering what will you be, what will you do, what difference will you make to others in this world? As Sam is unique, we are all unique; however, what our minds are fed at impressionable ages can change the colours on life's canvas and how we view our lives. Sam arrived at our home, shy and timid after the rigours of farm life. Now he is relaxed, gentle and caring. Hard to imagine a world without Sam, for as we have changed colours in his paint-box he has also changed the colours in ours and people he met on his canvas of life. When the painting is complete, he will have left a legacy to many people, both young and old, family and stranger, of a unique life that has blessed many.

As each person's canvas is created, the colours change with the circumstance. Transitions from teenager to adult, travel, marriage and the myriad of life's adventures as we progress day to day. Sometimes other people, friends or family, paint colours on our canvas without permission and there is little we can do about it. We can't remove the paint, so we need to add our own colours, replacing their brush strokes with colours that will enhance our life, altering colours that are neither beneficial nor fruitful to our lives. Not always easy to do. Family members can challenge your integrity, business partners may choose to steal from you and the list can go on. Ceasing work on the canvas or closing the paint box during difficult times is not what Jesus wants, as now could be a time for a new bold palette and brushstrokes on your canvas. *"He has made everything beautiful in its time" (Ecclesiastes 3:11 NIV).*

Of all the challenges and circumstances of life that muddy paintbox colours, rendering them useless to the owner so their canvas remains incomplete, is the act of bullying. This is a pretty hot topic these days appearing not only in the workplace but also in government-run institutions, local councils and homes for the aged as well as schools. Due to the advent of social media, the school playground has increased in size, making children and young people targets of destructive behavioural comments affecting a young person's life forever.

As a child, my parents moved from a city to a country town and I experienced first-hand what a rough school can dish out. Actions in a small community school for a child carry through into the neighbourhood, and as we all lived in the vicinity of the school, the neighbourhood became an extension of the school playground. Silver linings come in many forms and I learned to stand, irrespective of circumstance, on my own two feet (later in life I sort the Lord's help!) in life's rough seas and storms. However, the remnants of such experiences change the palette of colours in your paintbox with feelings of anxiety and constant searching of the horizon for storms that may never arise, believing they need your attention.

Many years later, when I met Linda and we started a family, my daughter who was attending a private school experienced constant verbal and physical abuse. A crisis point was reached and the day came for her to be removed since the school had no bullying policy. One parent at the school suggested she toughen up or get out and I am relieved she got out. Her education reports showed a performance way below her par and ability. Colours in her paintbox had changed and almost dried up, but through God's love and grace, her passion for horses, she completed her education by correspondence and now prospers in every aspect of her life.

Some people will say, "Well this is the way the world is, life's unfair, get over it?"

Unfortunately, a more sinister nature develops when power is abused to discriminate against age, race, belief or skin colour. Unimaginable atrocities are being performed in this world due to the latter. There is no intention on my part to undermine the word genocide by making the comparison with bullying; however, both start with intimidation. Policymakers in governments and public institutions who will not or cannot help dispossessed people will see them stand on their own two feet, eventually seeking ways to deal with the situation themselves. A unanimous vote for Israel to be a home for the Jews was passed in 1947 by the United Nations. Upon this announcement, delegates from Arab states staged a walkout threatening to drive the citizens of this newly ordained nation into the sea. Arab League leader Abdul Rhaman Azzaman stated 'a war of extermination and momentous massacre' would occur should the state of Israel go ahead; it still did. Six months later on the eve of the 14th May 1948, Israel's day of state independence, Palestinian Arabs followed by Lebanon, Syria, Trans-Jordan and Egypt attacked the fledgling nation. Israeli troop casualties totalled 6373, of which 2000 were Holocaust survivors. These statistics represented one percent of the nation's population from a race of people seeking independence and freedom from persecution. A fairly good reason for any country to develop one of the most formidable military forces in the world. I am not advocating a moral high ground on a complex topic as this would be incorrect. However, we must review history and scripture for the reasons and the outcomes to qualify the decisions made by countries such as Israel. The goals of terrorism and bullying are the same, being political or personal intimidation. Cowardly acts that are spiritually fuelled actions designed to coerce, torment and persecute with solutions only found by trusting God and seeking His help in these situations.

A sixteen-year-old boy's sandals kick up the dust as he walks down to the plain in the Valley of Elah. Clothed in a rough homespun garment, he carries with him a piece of leather and five smooth stones for a standoff with one of the world's first recorded bullies. Goliath, resplendent in armour, with sword, spear and shield, presents a formidable picture of power and strength, an example of modern-day sabre-rattling and intimidation. David declares to him, *"You come against me with sword and spear and javelin, but I come against you in the name of the LORD Almighty, the God of the armies of Israel, whom you have defied" (1 Samuel 17:45 NIV).* David's whirring sling releases the stone, which, travelling at over sixty miles per hour, flew into world history declaring the outcome of this shepherd boy's faith.

David the son of Jess, a humble shepherd boy, the future King of Israel, both warrior, psalmist, musician and military tactician, gave God a free hand on his canvas of life. Let us ensure God is part of our colours and brush strokes just as David inquired of him long ago.

Any masterpiece is lavished with love, passion and great attention to detail and just as David, the Apostles and others trusted Jesus with their canvas of life, it is because they 'would' and not 'should'.

Recently, while looking at some amazing clouds and rays of light, my wife Linda said, "They are like God's eyelashes and the light coming through is His Glory." I had never thought about it that way!

Colours we will use change with everyday situations and for faith, wisdom and humility to be prevalent on the canvas, our relationship with Jesus is essential. When children paint, the ideas are simple, uncomplicated, bold and transparent works of art. Genuine expressions of their experiences, who they are and their surroundings. When we paint, we need to use colours such as compassion, love, mercy, truth, grace, selflessness and generosity in large brush strokes. For what does the Lord require of us, *"To act justly and to love mercy and to walk humbly with your God" (Micah 6:8 NIV).*

What a masterpiece will that canvas be.

Once a Story Is Told
It Can but Grow Old

"The announcement and story to mankind of
Jesus Christ remains unchanged."

ONCE A STORY IS TOLD (IT CAN BUT GROW OLD):

Roses do, people do, Sam will and so will you and I. Children Sam has met on our journey will grow up, complete high school, next they have their driver's licence, attend university and the story of their lives truly begins. A journey of transformation from adolescence into adulthood. What they will do, where they achieve or fail, as a story remains untold as only a few chapters have been written and the open road lies ahead of them?

Every day, the news changes, and the speed of communication accelerates. What took months or weeks by ship one hundred years ago is delivered into our living rooms via the world message system hanging on a wall for all to see. Our minds are not only indulged and exposed to brands and the desires of every possible whim of the world, but also there is no shortage of tragedies and depravity. This leaves many of us shocked and speechless. Most news coverages are stories of 'selfishness' and not 'selflessness', showing greed, exploitation and intolerance. Each day being replenished with more of the same, as yesterday is old news and viewer impact has diminished and needs to be refreshed for better ratings.

Check out your street, place of work, neighbours and acquaintances, and see what life stories they have to share. Some years ago, on a training run in New Zealand, I passed an older man with two walking sticks struggling to close a farm gate. Offering my assistance, he was amazed and relieved that someone would help as he was recovering from recent knee replacements. During my conversation with this robust ninety-year-old, he shared his time in the French Foreign Legion! There are stories in all of us and I am certain parents wonder how the chapters of their children's lives will evolve as they move from schooling into adulthood and greater responsibilities. Pages to be turned for this next generation of our families and friends are yet to be written, as we do not know the screenplay for their book of life, nor do the participants.

The announcement and story to mankind of Jesus Christ through (*John 3:16*) was pre-ordained and will never grow old. Somewhere, every day in the world, this announcement is proclaimed in some form, language, place and time. Of all the news and stories recorded and repeated throughout world history, this message remains unchanged. Facts, experience and announcements by witnesses, both old and new, call them reporters if you may, report and declare the same story. Historically, no other documented event has a 'forward' written seven hundred years or more before the actual occurrence, with future events matching the minutest detail. Although the episodes and incidents coincide with the forward in consistency, depth and accuracy, many readers are still reluctant to accept the title of the author!

Content, substance and validation centuries before through the Psalms of David and by prophets Isaiah and Jeremiah, expounding the coming of Jesus Christ, have remained unchanged. Papyrus, parchment, clay tablets, paper and ink have been part of the process to record these events with technology now taking the 'good news' to a new platform. A message now being available to people throughout the world in their living rooms and on many other electronic devices. Why, then, with so many resources available and ease of access, are today's governments and institutions not embracing the information? Jesus the man was an 'inconvenient truth' during the time of Israel's Roman occupation and the ripple effects of his ministry, rocked both Pharisees and Roman rule to the core. Although a tolerable relationship between these governing and religious parties had developed, they failed miserably to serve the people to whom they were ultimately responsible. History, unfortunately, repeats itself and the yeast that pervaded the bread then, pervades our society and leadership today.

Policymakers of Christian countries are well aware that our man-made laws have been developed on Greek Judean principles of democracy and Christian values. School and education are compulsory so future generations can make informed decisions about their futures and create a better world. All of these are highly commendable. We are asked and taught to respect human rights and not to deny young people in schools the principles of our value system (Christian based). Still, most education appears to only ever cater to the mind and the body. Are we saying there is no soul or spirit?

America's finest neurosurgeon, Ben Carson, claimed that the more he studied the human mind, the more he believed in the Creator and the human spirit. We boast volumes about the spirit of our nation – a collection of people with spirit – the spirit with which we play a sport and therefore feed future generations a spiritual legacy where the author remains incognito.

Any story can be handed down orally and with many cultures, this was the primary method of retaining history, identity and their ancestral heritage. Although many shared verbally from generation to generation, there are also hieroglyphics and writings for us to study and observe mankind from previous centuries. Jesus' story, however, is handed down not only in the written word but also in spirit with the power to transform lives. Whereas archaeology frequently finds new evidence predating existing information, God's personal sacrifice of his son (Jesus) has never changed. Being born into very humble circumstances, Jesus was guided and filled with the spirit of his heavenly Father. Both his life and three-year ministry being one of 'selflessness' and 'servanthood'. God gave to the earth, he carefully created, an opportunity for all to share in his Son's story. Media coverage about Jesus' miracles, hopes, signs and wonders continue because this story never grows old due to the implications and evidence. Others have actively challenged it and stated that the Bible contradicts itself but fail to consider when the apostles were observing Christ's ministry, they would not have always viewed or listened from identical locations. Logically, subtleties in reports on any event will differ slightly. Many of today's reporters use different phraseology or words to describe an event, ultimately, the message content they all present is the same.

People who have read the story of Jesus have often said this is not for me, taking no further steps. By necessity, God's word, appears to challenge the world value system. None of us are perfect and God has made us well aware, wanting you and I to pursue this further. Surveys indicate a large number of people believe there is life after death and many believe there is heaven and hell. Some simply don't know. So, what do we know? *"For God so loved the world that he gave his one and only Son, that whoever believes in him shall not perish but have eternal life" (John3:16 NIV)*. This is a call to relationship with God because we ALL fall short of God's requirements to spend eternity with him. To impute our lives with forgiveness, a credit to the value of his Son's life and sacrifice has been distributed. How precious is your own son? Obviously, this is a God that does not demand, but one that loves abundantly. *Selah.*

Some wonderful everyday people struggle with the story of Jesus, why I am not sure, since such compelling evidence and facts point the way. Countries of privilege such as Australia and New Zealand, due to their natural abundance, possibly create a false impression for the necessity of God in everyday life; the answer is so close to those who are far away. *"But God chose the foolish things of the world to shame the wise; God chose the weak things of the world to shame the strong" (1Corinthians 1:27 NIV).*

Life's adventures can be a roller coaster, with serious G forces. As a young person at either high school or commencing university, I am certain that you want life's adventure to count. Personally, I also want it to count with the story of your life being as great as God desires for you. Partner with Jesus. He will open doors and close doors, sustain and deliver you with a foundation of grace and wisdom and mercy, all ingredients of His legacy and gift to you. Your story in Him will not grow old growing in chapter and events, trials, failures and successes with victory ultimately waiting for you.

One day, you will say as I did.

I asked the Lord at night do I have victory? He replied you have victory in Me.

The Distance Between Us

"Relationships require all parties to walk
shoulder to shoulder sharing successes and failures."

THE DISTANCE BETWEEN US:

*The crisp morning is invigorating. Our neighbour's horses lift their heads to observe me momentarily, only to carry on grazing. Blue sky has replaced yesterday's rain clouds, which came late this year and the green of the pastures in the valley has finally returned. Temporarily lost in thought, I realise my furry pal Sam is not ten metres in front but fifty metres behind! Preoccupied and snuffling along the grass, checking who may have claimed ownership of his favourite road sign, not realising how the distance between us has grown. 'Come on, Sam, **get a move on**' something registers and with a joyful wag of his tail, he starts running, catching me up.*

Distance is both mental and physical; young men and women may be called to serve their country far from loved ones, and people whose careers, such as airline pilots, are taken far from home regularly to other parts of the globe. Time and place may separate, but the 'mental' keeps them close to home and their families. When relationships break down, we may be walking together nearby, but mentally and spiritually, we have become separated. This happens in homes, churches, at work, government parties, nations and with neighbours. Relationship breakdowns or train wrecks, whatever you wish to call them, all have a point of departure. For a marriage, company contract, trade agreement or friendship to have existed, people either came together out of natural and mutual affection for each other or have seen benefits in forming alliances observing the value in the other person and the potential relationship.

When fear, doubt, broken trust and greed have managed to have a party, relationship foundations start to implode and eventually crumble. Should genuine attempts to repair not be attended to, with tools of honesty, love, truth, humility and courage, the relationship will collapse completely. Distance between all of us is accentuated in day-to-day living with the busyness of life, technology and the constant use of modern communication systems. Picture a young couple dating for the first time, sitting at a restaurant table, and the guy sends the girl a text asking if she would prefer either red or white wine. I trust you get my point!

When Christ shared the parable of the Good Samaritan *(Luke 10:29–37),* insight can be gained by giving both time and location consideration. Samaria was not Judah's favourite neighbour. Samarians were considered idolaters, yet it was a person from Samaria who cared for the Jew left for dead by thieves on the Jerusalem to Jericho road. In the story, we are told a priest passed by on the other side, followed by a Levite who also comes from a priestly calling as well. Levites were destined to either serve in the tabernacle or actually become a priest. Failure for either priest or Levite to give assistance to a fellow countryman is difficult to comprehend, so let us dig more deeply into the story's circumstances. In those days, the road to Jericho from Jerusalem was a major trading route and the terrain, both narrow and winding, made it notoriously dangerous as it provided easy concealment for thieves and bandits. Physically, due to the narrow road width, both priest and Levite may have had to step over the injured man, making their attitudes appear even more heartless. Conjecture, has suggested it may have been a trick, therefore the Priest and the Levite were concerned thieves could still be hiding. However, the thieves *"They stripped him of his clothes, beat him and went away, leaving him half dead" (Luke10:30 NIV)* suggesting any close proximity of a 'passer-by' would have revealed the seriousness of the man's wounds.

Both priest and Levite did check the body. *"A priest happened to be going down the same road, and when he saw the man, he passed by on the other side. So too, a Levite, when he came to the place, and saw him, passed by on the other side" (Luke 10:31–32 NIV)*. Did their piety and social station prevent them from assisting with this unfortunate? So, a man from Samaria, a people frowned upon and shunned, came to the aid of their countryman? Whatever their reasons, both priest and Levite passed by on the other side, creating distance between themselves and God as well as the problem. We walk at a distance when we do not want to be involved, because involvement requires some level of personal sacrifice. When you visit a friend or stranger in hospital, you have to travel in a car, pay for parking – most likely at the end of a busy workday, you may make gifts of fruit, all of which require sacrifice on your behalf, as did the Good Samaritan.

We have all walked at a distance sometime in our lives. Just like Sam, we were distracted and took our eyes off the ball. One of the saddest and most remarkable cases in history is the story of the apostle Peter. I believe Peter, of all the apostles, was always the first to do anything, first to recognise Christ as the Messiah, first to step out of the boat when called, the first man to visit the empty tomb, generally outspoken and brash he had the Nike philosophy 'just do it' written all over him. In the garden of Gethsemane before Christ's trial, the disciples slept while Jesus sweated blood and agonised over pending events and when arrested, the team fled. *"But Peter followed him at a distance, right up to the courtyard of the high priest. He entered and sat down with the guards to see the outcome"* (Matthew 26:58 NIV).

Two things will make us follow at a distance: fear and doubt. When fearful, we are reluctant to be involved or act and doubt shows a lack of confidence both in ourselves and others preventing us from acting. CS Lewis observed that the human mind is not *"completely ruled by reason,"* our emotions therefore participating in the decision-making process. When emotions join the decision-making committee, rational and reason will disappear and we may follow at a distance, as we saw with Peter. Crossroads are tough places, and any distance in our relationship with Jesus will force you to check the signpost carefully before proceeding. With Peter, his crossroads were temporary, Jesus restored him *(John 21:15–17),* and this remarkable person made an amazing come back from both fear and failure after denying the Son of God.

Relationships require all parties to walk shoulder to shoulder, sharing successes and failures, burdens, grief, adventures and life. Walking at a distance will be of little benefit either to you or your partner in life or in your relationship with Christ, as the best seat is up the front in any concert. Some children seek seats at the back of the class, hoping they will not be asked to interact with the teacher or class. Maybe they wish to read another book or it is simply a subject and class they don't enjoy; the teacher will eventually entrust them with some task so they will realise they have not gone unnoticed.

Walking at a distance reduces our potential and deprives us of what could be rightfully ours in our lifetime. When we hang back we will never know what we could have achieved. A few years ago, I commenced a dive course with final certification to be completed in Fiji. After an initial close-up encounter with a white tip reef shark I was faced with running out of air while submerged. We had been down for a while and I knew we should be heading for a decompression depth. Indicating to my instructor that my air supply was low, my instructor gave me the 'OK' sign and continued swimming.

I followed him closely as he continued to point out various fish types and other coral reef marvels, but no plan to ascend for decompression was apparent. Pointing to my regulator, I made the 'T' sign again, he gives me the 'OK' continuing to conduct his wonderful underwater tour of marine life. To my dismay, after another glance at the regulator, there was zero air left in my tank. Suddenly, we break the surface, and we are now standing in a few feet of water. My smiling Fijian instructor had decompressed us on a gradual slope, while submerged. In the turquoise depths, there was no way I would let him out of site as my tank was well into the red, another good reason for not travelling at a distance with Christ. You may need some air!

Leaders who walk at a distance with their staff and colleagues will not progress as do team members who also choose to stand back. Technology has allowed us to achieve many things by remote control; most of my business is conducted that way due to overseas relationships. Even with the availability of Skype, formulating solid relationships is a serious challenge; there is still a barrier due to the distance between us. Over long distances, you can't have a coffee with someone in 'five' down the road, and there is an intangible relational chemistry in mankind that technology is unable to reproduce. Endless reliance, by current generations using technical innovation for communication, creates distance and separation where there should be none. Giving rise to many other social and relational issues. Relationships start at the coal face and develop; here, people endure, share challenges and risks, and grow together. We are all required at the coal face and Christ illustrated that very clearly in his ministry.

Attitudes of entitlement within work and organisational environments benefit no one as leadership by example functions only when our sleeves are rolled up. Our presence is required at the coal face with Christ, in mind, body and spirit, not talking or thinking about it. Very often, this is our default, when we walk at a distance.

For we are God's handiwork, created in Jesus Christ to do good works, which God prepared in advance for us to do, (Ephesians 2:10 NIV).

A Certain Place

"Whatever place you are in there is a place of the meeting, where there is neither condemnation nor judgement."

A CERTAIN PLACE:

As I close the gap to the top of the hill, Sam picks up the pace and on arrival, I turn to view the valley that falls away below us. Someone is training in the park below, a beautiful macaw to fly from their hand and then return. The bird's stunning plumage, in colours of blue and gold, flash iridescent in the sunlight, contrasting sharply with olive-coloured trees and the green grass. Sam has trotted on ahead over the gentle rise to the end of the cul-de-sac, where he will race the three Great Danes to the end of their fence line. Our return trip is accompanied by the sweet scents from lantana and other unidentifiable fauna and flora. At the base of the hill, all I can hear is my own breathing and the slap of track shoes on the road. This is Sam's and my place – a certain place.

There is a certain place for all of us in our relationship with God that will move us from the craziness of life's day-to-day routine allowing us to step into a realm of 'green pastures and still waters'. Church on Sunday is a place of learning for like-minded people from different walks to share and encourage in faith; however, it is only a step in the relationship you choose to form with Jesus. Our personal ongoing work during the week in the relational process of seeking God and what he wants for our lives is just as important. As his desires and will is assigned to us, we need to follow through.

Initially, I was surprised at the degree of one-on-one time God spent with me on my walks with Sam. Eventually, I posed the question, why? "Why would I not spend time with you when you spend much time seeking me out?" was the answer I was given. In *John 10:27 NIV*, it is written, *"My sheep listen to my voice; I know them, and they follow me".* Also, Jerimiah the prophet wrote *"You will seek me and find me when you seek me with all your heart" (Jerimiah 29:13 NIV).*

A dear friend of mine from New Zealand loves it when someone rings up and says, "How are you and the family?" Although the conversation may only be a brief one, the fact you bother to pick up the phone, creates the two-way relationship, and the person knows you care. Our potential for a one-on-one relationship with God came through Jesus, *"who has qualified you" (Colossians 1:12 NIV)* through the cross and his resurrection, to be partakers of our inheritance here and now. A certain place amidst our daily routines, challenges of living and life's journey.

The three wise men, astrologers and mathematicians, commenced a fact-finding journey, ending with an eventual encounter with Jesus. Considerable speculation has gone into these stories: from how many people there actually were, did they travel on camels as depicted or did they ride on horses? Considering the value of the gifts and goods they were carrying, protection of an armed escort whilst travelling in such lawless times, you would have to consider a necessity. Christmas tradition always depicts a baby in a manger surrounded by shepherds and the three wise men. In *Matthew 2:11*, the wise men meet with a young child (Jesus) and his mother in a house, appearing to be a slightly later date. *"On coming to the house, they saw the child with his mother Mary, and they bowed down and worshipped him"*. The Three Wise Men's journey and commitment to seek answers culminated in reaching a certain place. Since they knew they would be meeting 'royalty', they came prepared, having brought gifts of gold, frankincense and myrrh. Their way of blessing and offering praise. Each day we need to prepare gifts of thanks and praise as we seek him and should not be surprised at the small clear voice confirming our arrival at the destination.

The Bible is full of ordinary people arriving in certain places experiencing the presence of God.

Moses, while shepherding his father-in-law's sheep, isolated in the Midian, has a one-on-one with God when he observed the burning bush and approached it *(Exodus 3:2)*. Under the oak tree at Ophrah, belonging to Joash, Gideon's father, Gideon experienced the presence of the angel of the LORD *(Judges 6:11–23)*.

A wonderful Christian friend, helped me with rehab by insisting on cycling with me, helping to restore both fitness and health to previous levels. The acts of this Good Samaritan produced the much-needed physical and spiritual restoration after my illness. A common denominator in all of the examples is the presence of the Holy Spirit in the circumstance – a certain place. For the more Jesus is made part of our lives, the greater the relationship will be.

People go from certain places and circumstances to a certain place being singular and not plural as seen with the return of the prodigal son *(Luke 15: 11–32),* who after leaving for another country to indulge himself in riotous living, was finally forced to return home. Realising, he needed the security and certainty of his caring and loving father. When King David, on a spring evening, observed from his rooftop Bathsheba bathing, he was not where he usually would have been, for it was *"in the spring, at a time when kings go off to war" (2 Samuel 11 NIV).* In the physical, David should have been with his army, but in his mind, he was removed from his duties and responsibilities. An affair with the beautiful Bathsheba and the murder of her husband, his most trusted commander and friend, resulted from this place on the rooftop. Very sobering! How did David, the man after God's own Heart *(Acts 13:22)* get it so wrong? He had moved from a certain place of assurance with God to other places of the world. Our eyes being the windows of our soul consume, so we must look upon good things such as God's written word and then we are taken to a place of assurance, a place He wants us to be, close to Him.

Closeness and the reduction of distance are achieved only through communication and the method given by Jesus is through prayer and reading His word. If it makes you feel better by calling prayer a phone plan, go for it; however, more effort will be required than dialling a number or sending a text. The upside is, you don't get sorry this mailbox is full, or can I call you back. Happens a lot, as some recipients only consider the 'me' benefits rather than what can I do for you.

A certain place is promised and assured when *"Whoever dwells in the shelter of the Most High will rest in the shadow of the Almighty" (Psalm 91:1 NIV).* A place of shelter and grace has been prepared and we can rest in the knowledge of his protection in a place of peace and calm. His shadow that covers us is more than sufficient and the greatness of His presence is behind it. Call the shadow your daily bread (spiritually), trusting with great faith the Grace that towers behind it, for we have been given a certain place. Go there without compromise and reserve nothing, approaching with humility and an open heart, as Moses did with the burning bush and the magi did also in their search for the King of Peace.

When I lace up my track shoes, pick up Sam's lead and head down our driveway, I often wonder what God will share with me today?

Post Script:

Cabin fever has set in after a week of rain, bound to the office and spread between business duties and writing this chapter. We wake, however, to a new day with sunshine and clear skies, and it's time for Sam and I to hit the road. With renewed energy, we set the pace and during our progress, '*will rest in the Shadow of the Almighty*' came clearly to mind. At this time of day, I cast a reasonably long shadow; however, an additional shadow much larger than mine stretched up the road before us, moving wherever we went. The shadow, simply being longer and almost transparent in appearance. With 'Rest in the shadow of the Almighty' ringing in my head, Sam and I continued our walk.

This route, Sam and I have done countless times. Why am I surprised and amazed? Is it a pilgrimage of faith spread over years, you can decide? For me, it is about a place of rest with God. As I have shared about certain places, in the story of Moses in *Exodus 33:22 NIV: "when my glory passes by, I will put you in a cleft in the rock, and will cover you with My hand till I have passed by"* he (Moses) was in a certain place spiritually and I truly hope you do not give up on your quest for Jesus' presence and place in your life.

We know from the scripture, during the crucifixion, there was a darkening of the earth for a considerable period before Jesus died. Those who loved and followed him stood in the shadow, figuratively or possibly literally, of the Almighty. They had come to a certain place, the embodiment of God's power, grace and love for all humanity that would follow millions of Christians worldwide for thousands of years to come and still does today. This book, I believe, has now arrived at a certain place, and I have a better understanding of why I am writing and why the project was placed so heavily on my heart.

Whatever place you are in, there is a place of the meeting, where there is no condemnation or judgment, a place of rest and great shelter in the shadow of the Almighty.

Message in a Bottle

"Feeding the inner man is not just the best dagwood sandwich you are about to consume, it is feeding the thing that makes you tick, your spirit, with good food."

MESSAGE IN A BOTTLE:

Ears up, ears down, sad eyes, happy face, Sam's range of expressions are unlimited, for whatever he lacks vocally, one cannot misinterpret what he communicates visually. Recent studies have revealed that our canine family members recognise not only the tonality of a person's voice but many more words than previously thought. For Sam, commands are not lost in translation however varied the method of communication, which can either be by word, body language, sensitivity or touch.

Over the last few weeks, a client of mine has commenced outsourcing work to Vietnam and certain difficulties have arisen due to expectations not being met. Client confidence has diminished rapidly and a search for a new supplier is underway as dramatic changes are needed on the existing supplier's part. Internal communication systems are the key issues, as instructions to senior management are relayed to customer service teams, who in turn relay them to the staff responsible for the project. When you add, into the mix, translation from English to Vietnamese things can prove a challenge, as the authenticity of the message becomes blurred. Outcomes on deliverables continued to be below par as client instructions were not followed or missed and similar problems repeated themselves continuously with ongoing projects.

In the past, I have regularly heard comments expressed: The Old Testament is boring, the Bible is full of contradictions and there is no application any more for modern man. Being dismissive when you read a copy for the first time is not totally unreasonable, considering the message shared is by men and women from thousands of years ago. Firstly, the Bible cannot be considered just any other book, to be read and understood as a great story, with fictitious characters, within a two-dimensional frame. A third lens needs to be applied when reading. Goals from the author (God) to the reader are to communicate relationship, teaching, wisdom, love, admonishment, compassion, grace and mercy. This sounds very much like any parent to me. Countless everyday people were used by the author, from a broad tapestry of backgrounds, to convey his thoughts and instructions and to complete His book for mankind. People chosen for these tasks wrote from their personal experience and communication with the author using a third lens. Through this lens, we need to view chapters and events expressed in both Old and New Testaments and how they parallel each other. Today's world has changed little from the time of the scriptures, with many technical advances, but mankind's deeds and attitudes have not improved with those advances. We still have slavery, sex trade, wars, famine, corruption and greed at every level of society. Therefore, the application of scripture still applies today and will continue for aeons due to mankind's fallen nature.

World occurrences four thousand years ago sound very similar to your local and overseas news and channels. We are simply informed faster, in more depth and the general populace is now able to review information globally and assess its authenticity. For all the benefits of the world media, we are still subject to spin doctors, biased journalism built around identity values ('not true political party values'), so information is no longer impartial but relative. Information validity is vital just as creative accounting can weight balance sheets for potential shareholders; our social media influences and polls can manipulate people's viewpoints before a share release or vote. Lines between truth, fact or fiction have become increasingly blurred as editing of original information can change the original context.

Three Bedouin shepherds, in late 1946 and early 1947, discovered by accident the first of the Seven Dead Sea Scrolls in the Qumran Caves. Discoveries of this magnitude cannot be overemphasised, as earliest Bible manuscripts date from the ninth century 'after Christ' and copies before this have been lost. Additional searches, conducted through 1956, by teams of archaeologists, produced findings of over eight hundred full manuscripts along with thousands of fragments from the second century BC. Documentation was a thousand years older than any existing Hebraic scripture available before this discovery. For the next fifty years, texts were translated, the jigsaw puzzle of fragments painstakingly assembled and scholars found approximately five percent or less variation, when compared to existing Bible translations. Also, neither a single teaching nor doctrine had been altered, leaving us with a million-dollar question. Why nothing is lost in translation through the distance of time and language (Aramaic, Greek and Hebrew)? Something so complex as the writings of Isaiah, end-times prophecies of Daniel and many others. Because the book is divinely inspired by the author and those who wrote it had a relationship with Him.

Scripture expresses the relationship God has for the people of the world, and as any father desires only good things for his children, He is no different. We see this when Jesus was asked by a disciple in *Luke11:1–4* how to pray; apparently, this follower was uncertain how to approach God! Through 'The Lord's Prayer', as it became known, the relational aspect God wishes to have with each one of us is expressed in *Matthew 6:9-13 NIV*.

Our Father in heaven. There is a shift from God in the Old Testament to Father in the New Testament. We are instructed to call on our 'Father' (*Romans 8:15)* and there can be no confusion about the instruction as a stranger would not be referred to as 'Father'. For the word applies only to a person who was responsible for your existence, created you and holds your interests above all else.

We are reminded that his name is *hallowed*, revered and holy. We are, however, to call him Father and that permission comes through Jesus. When we know the Son (Jesus), the relationship changes from God to Father. Like the disciple who asked how to pray, he knew the Son Jesus, he could then pray accordingly.

Your kingdom come. We would rather Jesus reign on earth than the current world system, bringing us to the challenging verse *Your will be done, on earth as it is in heaven.* Implications of this are enormous; every thought decision and action we make, needs to be as it is done in heaven. Of all the level playing fields, this is it. When decisions fall into the grey area and answers are needed, I think of this instruction which challenges every human condition and how we choose to treat others in our homes, work, business and at places of learning.

Give us today our daily bread. We all need sustenance, food on an ongoing basis to function each day. When I was ill, Linda asked the specialist if there were any dietary requirements needed to counter the negative effects of intravenous antibiotics on my immune system. "Michael will need good F.O.O.D." We all burst out laughing, which was really painful as my healing was far from complete, but laughter is a great healer and I still smile when I think about it. Our daily sustenance is not built around our *bread alone;* it is also built around spiritual sustenance as well. Feeding the inner man is not just the best dagwood sandwich you are about to consume; it is feeding the thing that makes you tick, your spirit, with good food.

And forgive us our debts, as we also have forgiven our debtors. Everyone requires forgiveness in their lives. You are late for a work meeting, and the boss cuts you some slack because you were running the kids to school, this being a recurrence. Just remember to be understanding and forgiving when the boss gets staunch and stressed about this year's sales performance he has to present to his board. All everyday events; however, there are truly horrific situations in which people have forgiven others. Corrie ten Boom and Betsie, her sister, were sent to the notorious Ravensbruck concentration camp in WWII, where her sister passed away during their internment. After the war, she was speaking at a church in Munich when a grey-haired man from the audience stepped forward at the end of the service requesting her forgiveness. She recognised him as one of the most brutal guards from Ravensbruck and then to make matters worse, he extended his hand for her to take. Amidst a flood of terrible emotions, she took his hand, and after a pause said, "I forgive you brother with all my heart." A truly remarkable woman.

And lead us not into temptation, but deliver us from the evil one – circumstances, friends and even hardship can tempt us where God will never test us. Such circumstances that challenge us can be the catalyst for unwise choices; we, however, need to stay on track and trust Him however difficult, to gain the outcomes He wants for us. This is a place of standing and letting *His grace be enough this day.*

When information is lost in translation, clarity and order go out the door, which is not the way God works for He has inspired men divinely in history for thousands of years. We also have a bunch of earthenware jars as confirmation for both the believer and the non-believer, as a reminder of how the greatest men from the cradle of civilisation knew the living God. Many today choose to deny His existence, as they are not truthful to themselves. I believe it would be better if they said, "I am simply not interested," for we cannot make an informed decision of the existence of the Living God, His Word and the Work of His only begotten Son through our own self-denial.

The meaning of the translations is complete – nothing has been lost in translation – only to those who do not read them.

Travel with Your Bags Packed

"Any journey on the road with Jesus is infinite
for you and your family,
as he is the Alpha and the Omega."

TRAVEL WITH YOUR BAGS PACKED:

On spindly legs and under the proud and watchful eye of the mare, the newborn foal raises itself, tentatively, testing the strength of its legs. Within thirty minutes, the foal was moving well, gaining strength minute by minute and finally coming to suckle for the first time. All of our Lord's creations are prepared for the journey and environment they are destined for, from the moment of birth. Even Sam, pacing back and forth impatiently, as I change into my running shorts and top before our walk. Finally, to his relief, I lace up my track shoes. How unprepared are we compared to the rest of His creation?

Years spent on the road moving one hundred kilos of photography equipment (or more) onto planes for national or international travel meant I needed to know without any doubt each case was securely and correctly packed. Success of projects, which in turn meant future business opportunities, depended on detailed preparation. Our family lawyer, a blessing both professionally and as a friend, shared with me his Christian perspective after my plane fiasco. 'We all need to travel with our bags packed', this analogy could not have been better, for so many years of my life had been spent packing and unpacking bags. His wisdom, which remained with me for years, even after I came to Christ, compels me to share its value with you.

Our greatest oversight is not observing life as a journey and after receiving a boarding pass, knowing we *must* arrive at the destination. Where this place is, at what point in the future, the how and where, only our Lord knows. Experienced travellers understand the importance of preparation, having the correct documentation, reducing their luggage essentials to a minimum for ease of airport transfers, limiting possible unwanted delays. Some nations require citizens from another country to have a visa granting permission for you to cross their borders and should you make a false declaration or carry prohibited goods, you will be turned away.

Jesus prepared the documentation of life for you in the New Covenant, which is spoken of as the 'perfect law of liberty' in *James 1:25*. A covenant is an agreement, promise and undertaking by one party to another. The crucifixion and resurrection of Jesus unpacked the bag of mankind's sin, giving all an opportunity to repack it should we believe in Him, honouring what He has done through the Father for us.

We all seek security for our families and naturally work hard and pray we can leave them financially secure. Burgeoning insurance companies, play to our insecurities and offer insurance for, house, car, valuables, loss of profit, income protection, life, health, partnership, public liability, tax audit policies and the plethora of categories are still growing. We all spend up large with companies offering these services and within reason, it may be wise to do so. Origins of insurance companies go back four thousand years to the Babylonian Empire, where it was designed to protect loans on maritime cargo. One of the challenges to any insurance policy is your investment value and realisation of the investment exists only at the time of a claim! The expectations of the claimant and the insurance company will always differ. You as the claimant seek the policy to be honoured in the hour of your need, whereas some insurance companies *could* seek to either reduce the value of the claim or not pay at all. The fine print is there for a reason – any monetary value invested on your part is limited to a claim for an event, but not so with God.

When you first unpack the 'bag of your life' before Jesus, you are claiming what has already been prepared in advance for you – the imputations to your account are already there. Through His sacrifice and resurrection, your claim has already been settled, even before presentation. *"For I will forgive their wickedness, and will remember their sins no more"* (*Hebrews 8:12 NIV*).

Every dream and plan for life requires preparation; they also require guidance and direction. Dusty footprints of Jesus travels on the rough roads of Galilee did not depart forever, as did the spirit of God which hovered over the earth in Genesis, and we become a home (each person) for the Holy Spirit when we choose Christ. In *John 16:13* NIV, Christ tells us, *"But when he, the Spirit of truth, comes, he will guide you into all truth. He will not speak on his own; he will speak only what he hears, and he will tell you what is yet to come"*. God shares with us through the Holy Spirit, remember the small clear voice Elijah heard, do not be distracted and listen carefully for this and the mighty plan God has for your life.

The New Covenant is simple and as the mediator (Jesus) only asked in return, faith and trust, there is no fine print to wade through. None of us get it right one hundred percent of the time. We will try. I have failings just like any other person and that is why the bag has to be repacked. Let us look for the best in each other, as does Jesus in us, looking at the heart and not the external – the front to the world.

Today's times have an uncertainty that is more prevalent than any other period in the history of mankind. This is not a lesson on end times eschatology, but at the time of writing, Iran is bent on self-destruction and taking the world with it. As a child, Dad, Mum and my sister went to a neighbour's home specifically to watch the evening news on TV as our family did not own one. Being one of the few TVs in the area at the time, Dad had asked our neighbour if we could drop by at 7:00 pm that evening to watch this important news announcement. The evening was in October 1962 and President Kennedy's presentation on the Cuban Missile Crisis and the agreement reached with President Krushev of the Soviet Union was being broadcast. Some consider this to be the closest point in history to WWIII and to nuclear holocaust. Fifty years later, details of a speech surfaced, written in advance by President Kennedy, authorising the attack on the Russian missile installations in Cuba with conventional weapons. Obviously, this speech had been prepared before any final agreement with the USSR and President Kennedy's announcement to the world, to which our family had listened.

When you read between the lines all these years later, I know why my father was so worried.

Irrespective of the rumblings in the world and the turmoil that surrounds us, that is not the goal of travelling with your bags packed. Should you wish to know more, I suggest you read Joel Rosenberg's 'Epicentre' – Rosenberg is an authority on such matters writing with impartiality and from a truly Christian perspective. We are talking about end games, but there are a lot of fields to play in life's journey in the interim. When we recognise God as the officiator of the overall plan, we pack our bags according to His wishes, governments and nonbelievers need to, Christians also. As believers, we need to give serious consideration to what God wants for us, so let's turn off our iPhones and spend time with Him.

Our final destination for each man and woman is the close of life when we leave this world. I have had a wonderful travelling companion all these years, even in the times when I chose not to acknowledge Jesus. I firmly believe He was always present. Any journey on the road with Jesus is infinite for you and your family, as He is the Alpha and the Omega.

In recent years, Sam has been my constant on-road companion and part and parcel of the team and themes of this book. Sam's bag is always packed, and I am asking you to allow someone to help pack your bag for you. His name is Jesus Christ, Son of God, a carpenter, raised by Joseph and Mary in Galilee, descendants of the Hebraic tribe of Benjamin and the line of David.

A wonderful family and a great address.

In a Word

"The spoken word has life attached to it."

IN A WORD:

Power words, power ties, power suits and colours are the way of the sophisticated world. On a more down-to-earth note, the most powerful word in our house is 'game'. The saying let sleeping dogs lie is very true, mention the word 'game', and there is a rush for the door, a clamouring of yelps, whines, pushing and shoving for the first to get through so the ball throwing can begin.

It may seem contradictory to be writing about the power of 'a word' after years in the imaging business when many consider a photo worth a thousand words. A saying, based on a thousand written words versus a single image, this could well be the case; the spoken word is something very different.

Great orators know the secret to deliver a message and this is revealed in the parables shared by Jesus to his disciples. Parables did not give his disciples an immediate answer; instead, it challenged their thinking. Their personal evaluation and confirmation of the parable gave them a better answer and a greater understanding. Call it the silence between the notes that make a melody. Jesus' spoken words breathed life into the disciples' lives and we need to understand how this small organ in our bodies has so much power in day-to-day life.

Jesus' brother James compares the tongue to the rudder of a mighty ship, controlling its direction *(James 3:4)*. Even in storms, cross currents, and high winds, a rudder directs the ship to the predetermined destination. The spoken word has life attached to it, for as we speak, we breathe, our thoughts being translated into words to communicate situations, desires and commands. Like the movements of the rudder of a ship, words create the course of our direction.

How we breathe life into any situation is dependent on what comes from our mouth, the words we use, hence the expression 'let's breathe some life into it'. At the commencement of each verse *(3, 6, 9, 11, 14, 20, 24,)* in *Genesis 1NIV*, it is written *"And God said"* the power of His word was spoken and that which was formless, became creation and came into existence. In *Ezekiel 37:3–4 NIV*, God presents the prophet with a vision, a valley of dry bones. God asked him, *"Son of man can these bones live?" I said, "Sovereign LORD, you alone know." Then he said to me, "Prophesy to these bones and say to them, Dry bones, hear the word of the Lord!"* Instead of God speaking into the situation, he passes authority to Ezekiel to do this in his name. With further instruction from God, Ezekiel says, *"So I prophesied as he commanded me, and breath entered them" (Ezekiel 37:10NIV)*.

We can speak and declare, through the power and grace of God, into life's situations and circumstances.

When we see the man in the power suit and tie, he is making a visual declaration of who is running the show, an external statement. When we make a verbal declaration to employees or students, they are aware of what is on your mind. When we declare with our mouths, in faith and the authority of God, that takes it to a whole new level. Recently, I asked the Lord how to deal with some recurring challenges in business and He said to rebuke them in My Name *mountains tremble – you have not seen the size of my God.* The Lord was telling me to surrender circumstances to Him by declaration. We cannot just think this; we need Christians to declare and speak out in the Son's Name. Any military commander does not *think* his platoon into action he has to command and instruct them to do so; otherwise, nothing will happen. When we declare in Jesus Name in faith, we are using a strategy of *offence* and not the *defence*, exactly the opposite of the world's plan for you.

Hateful rhetoric is common in our society between people and nations and is an absolute travesty of the human condition. Government administrators seek to illegalise speech of this nature, doing so only at a personal level and only between nations and theocracies they choose. As divisions in society have become more apparent due to the development of the global village, left-wing and right-wing ideology is being felt not only within a nation but worldwide. Policymaking of individual countries has a profound effect on their neighbours as well as globally. Currently, Israel is being threatened continually by their enemies to be wiped off the map (again!) and given the opportunity, her enemies will 'have a go'.

Unfortunately, the United Nations, along with some allies, send no signals to the provocateurs condemning such verbal rhetoric. In *James 3:5* NIV, *"Likewise, the tongue is a small part of the body, but it makes great boasts"*, and in verse 6, *"The tongue also, is a fire, a world of evil among the parts of the body,"* reminding us of the power of words and their declarations. Threatening and disruptive speech used on an international platform is supposed to invoke fear, like one child sending a bully text to another. They are truly misguided. Whatever their political motives, they cannot be viewed through a secular lens. Israel is biblical, and God's view on the matter is made clear in *Zechariah 9:8 NIV. "But I will encamp at my temple to guard it against marauding forces. Never again will an oppressor overrun my people, for now I am keeping watch".* For me, the scenario is like the playground bully saying to the new kid on the block, "I'm gonna run you outta town!"

"Nup, that's not happening," says the new kid. Our bullyboy is incensed, a freckled-faced, cheeky kid telling him what is going to happen on his patch! Rolling up his sleeves to give the 'kid' a lesson, he suddenly sees the kids' big brother and realises he has made a bad career move.

Endless vile threats, border skirmishes, and terrorism are part and parcel of Israel's everyday existence and are due to the words and declarations of the enemy.

For a discussion to evolve on the passages in the Quran exacerbating war against the Jews, Christians and mankind, would alone, be a book. There are many Muslims, I am sure, who do not necessarily follow this teaching. For Jews, Christians, Muslims and nonbelievers, this challenge to our world is unfortunately written. Words of this nature in the Quran can be read, taught, spoken and shared with impressionable minds and given life.

When certain nations, surrounding Israel, teach their children to hate, there is no surprise they gravitate quickly from throwing rocks, as seen on international broadcasts, to launching RPGs. Unfortunately, ideology is veiled, and the truth is distorted. The actions of terrorists are contradictory to the peaceful claims of Muslims who are also subject to their atrocities. With skilful use of media, militant theocracies with evil agendas seek to exploit these writings as a tool for government policy, ruling by fear and giving life verbally to the written word.

All dialogue can change when negative emotions take hold in the form of anger, disappointment, sadness and fear. Christians, however, can speak and declare aloud against these situations in God's name. An article I came across recently touched my heart and illustrated exceptional courage and faith. On June 25th, 2006, eighteen-year-old Eliyahu Asheri, a Jewish teenager, while waiting for a ride in the French Hill area of Jerusalem, was abducted and later murdered by Arab terrorists. Before executing him, he was asked if he had a final wish. Eliyahu requested a cup of water and then prayed the Shehakol (Jewish Blessing). *"Blessed are you Lord our God King of the Universe by whose word all things come to be."* According to his perpetrators, who were eventually captured, this prayer was made with great intent.

From Eliyahu's story, we see two very different spirits and their fruits. We have a young man full of grace, immense faith and love for God submitting totally to His Will. *"Love does not delight in evil, but rejoices with the truth. It always protects, always trusts, always hopes, always perseveres" (1 Corinthians 13:6-7)*. Those who murdered him would, with great reluctance, have to admit reasons for their act of Cain were seated in envy, jealousy and hate. *"And why did he murder him? Because his own actions were evil and his brothers were righteous" (1 John 3:12 NIV).*

Our words convey our learning and innermost thoughts, and convert into everyday actions, becoming the fruit of who we are. Positive words *and* declarations convey to your children how you love them, your team at work, what a great job they have done. They are powerful instruments bringing blessing to others' lives. Sometimes, a word is all that is needed to get someone through their day. Our tongues are great and wonderful things with the power to fan flames, start fires, or destroy and deceive; they also have the power to bless and heal.

Declaration of God's healing blessing is apparent in *Isaiah 55:10 NIV*, we are told rain and snow does not return to the heavens and are sent for a purpose to moisten the earth. Seeds will grow, crops will come forth and man is sustained and rewarded. Isaiah, concludes, how God's word will be complete in *55:11 NIV, "so is my word that goes from my mouth: It will not return to me empty, but will accomplish what I desire and achieve the purpose for which I sent it".*

Written seven hundred years before the birth of 'His Word', Jesus Christ.

Two-point four billion Christians in the world today have experienced the might of 'His Word'. As Jesus declared, referring to his resurrection, His temple would be built in three days. Thousands of years later, we are the result of that declaration.

As Christians, we must not doubt the power of words and declarations in Jesus' name in faith.

My faithful friend, Sam, is nudging me for a game, I must go.

A Wisp of Smoke

"So will the mists and veils in your life vanish under
the power of Jesus' hand."

A WISP OF SMOKE:

Contrails of magenta tinted grey smoke stretch across a background of pale cyan as afternoon transitions to early evening. A chill is now present in the air and cuts through my lightweight tracksuit top. Sam and I are on the homeward stretch just nearing the bend in the road, where the plovers' nest at this time of year. It has been a good walk. A great time spent in our Garden of Eden with the Lord.

The smoke patterns did not last long, even though there was only the barest hint of a zephyr. Like vapour trails from a plane, it eventually dissipates into the atmosphere, ceasing to exist. In Jesus' eyes, we are not vapour, a wisp of smoke to vanish in the evening breeze. From the day we are born, He has a plan for us all. Any smokescreen, as you know, will sting our eyes to tears making it hard to breathe, because of the barrier and veil it creates between the air needed to breathe and live. These veils come in many forms, tints and shades; addiction to drugs, sex, alcohol, gambling and many more, consuming people's lives and families. Other addictions do not carry the same social stigma, workaholics, social media, hatred and intolerance. Paul, the apostle who wrote two-thirds of the New Testament, persecuted the early Christian community, resorted to every trick in the book to bring believers, in chains or worse, before the authorities. Standing by, he watched as Stephen (the first Christian Martyr) was stoned to death. Addiction can take on many forms, which is why on the road to Damascus (Paul was called Saul at the time) Jesus transformed Saul's life *(Acts 9:1–19).*

When we look at Paul's maniacal attitude to Christendom, did it stem from fear and a lack of self-worth? According to scripture, he was an overachiever proud of his heritage as both Jew and a citizen of Rome. He had received exemplary training and had already attained great accomplishments. For a person so highly educated, it is difficult to comprehend why there was so much hate for Christians *(Acts 9:1).* Whatever the deepest reasons, Paul was consumed, obsessive and addicted to the goals he set for himself. Although you may not have the same experience as Paul did on the road to Damascus, both change and redemption, which he received, is available to all of us.

When Linda and I were first married, I was a smoker and our doctor offered me choices: running shoes or medication for my blood pressure, also kick the habit. I chose running shoes. On the first night, Linda and I went down to the park with the new running shoes I ran a lap of the sports field, it nearly killed me (to Linda's delight and amusement). With persistence, the smoking ceased, the weight vanished and I became extremely fit, finally entering in a half marathon. Our doctor gave me the right tools for stress management and to this day, my exercise regime is a vital part of my life. Looking back, even though I was not a Christian at the time, I realise now how Jesus will give you the right tools with which to run the race of life.

The veil or veils in your life separate you either completely or by degree from the blessings that God has for you. Our enemy in this life is the master of deceit and lies and he will give one hundred percent effort to the one percent that can hold you back. He will do anything to imprison you emotionally and physically, using tools of addiction and attacks on your self-worth.

I ask you, with compassion, how do you see yourself? You may be struggling, seeing limitations enforced on you, set by the grip of previous choices. Not only does Jesus see and is aware of your circumstances, He also knows what you can be in Him. In *Isaiah 49:16 NIV*, *"See, I have engraved you on the palms of my hands;"* expresses the immense value He places on each one of us. When He opens his hands, you are right there in front of him. Any addiction or learned behaviour places people in bondage; they are no longer free men or women. They may be wearing the hallmarks of freedom, but in truth, are as incarcerated as either Jews were in the time of Moses in Egypt or political prisoners in a gulag in Siberia.

When we conquer ourselves, we prepare ourselves to do great things and make the impossible possible. To do this, we call on the Jesus to speak against the bindings of our lives and '*let my people go*'. Words that have echoed through the millenniums. As God chose Moses to command the pharaoh, the same command can be part of your life as well. Pharaoh saw God's people as possessions, something to own, personal property, with no consideration for human life.

The king of lies, like the pharaoh, will use any tool of deception or excuse to hold you in bondage. Ten plagues later, all of them delivered on the people of Egypt, pharaoh released God's people and they were now free from his hand and power. As the Israelites were delivered from captivity, you can also be released by Jesus' hand of forgiveness, grace and power. Egypt's brutal regime for four hundred years had held God's people in bondage, now time was needed to heal after their release. God's pillar of fire by night and the cloud by day set the direction and Jesus will do the same for you in the form of healing, spiritual strength and a renewed life. Nothing has changed; trust Him and give him permission to start work in you.

Freedom of mind, body and spirit is hard won and people are held in bondage even in this day and age with naivety calling from the sideline, an imitation of freedom. Although apparent at personal levels, it is also at international levels. Terrorism binds people and nations just as drugs and other criminal rackets do. Two trillion dollars is the estimated cost of the 9/11 attacks, including post effects on stock market, tourism and the economy. When border control tightens to protect countries, tourism falls due to fear and uncertainty, a subtle form of bondage restricting movement and increasing costs, taxes and global compliance.

Our current generation lives in a world of uncertainty and disharmony with the fruit of strife apparent everywhere. Terribly discouraging for impressionable minds and the smaller the global village gets, the greater the effect on them. Solomon came to a conclusion that even with all his power and wealth, he could see little value in anything, yet concluded how valuable God was. Do not doubt His plan for you; it is not a life of mist or vapour but one of grace and great promise. *Psalm 139:16 NIV "Your eyes saw my unformed body; all the days ordained for me were written in your book before one of them came to be".*

Before you were born, you were created, and the Lord took time to write down all the great things he wanted for your life and yet your life had not begun. I would call this a movie script, starting with Take One, Scene One – your arrival in the world. Being a naturally inquiring person, you will want to know what the other scenes are. You need to ask Jesus and seek his direction for each of those scenes.

As the morning mist burns away with the heat of a rising sun, so will the mists and veils in your life vanish under the power of Jesus' hand.

On the Way Home

"Each life is a journey and gift to us by the living God."

ON THE WAY HOME:

Sam and I are New Zealand citizens proud of our heritage: the Silver Fern, All Blacks, Blackcaps, Black Magic (Americas Cup winning yacht) and pavlova. Our roots and hearts seated in the mountains, valleys, rivers and streams of our nation. Citizenship of New Zealand, for us both, is automatic along with the benefits and entitlements as we were born and raised there. Multicultural societies evolve when people from other nations and cultures immigrate for work or lifestyle reasons to another country. Qualification, for permanent residency in another homeland, is available via a criteria of conditions but actual citizenship is not automatically granted. This may come later. Although the transition is physical and overtime integration into a new society takes place, it is a paper transformation only. Neither a personal nor spiritual one.

After reading Exodus, at the age of thirteen, and other works by Leon Uris, such as Milla 18 and The Haj, I became fascinated with the Middle East. Israel somehow seemed to rise from the ashes and at the time I lived there, New Zealand's population was similar, approximately two point five million. As the years have rolled on to this present day, New Zealand has a population of four point five million and Israel nearly eleven million and climbing. Jews globally are returning to their homeland. For many years, I have wondered why this country has been a spiritual home to me. Possibly Israel's ingenuity and ability to rise to the top against overwhelming opposition and odds appealed to me.

Jerusalem is the spiritual home for Judaism and Christians alike, and as followers of Christ, we need to consider Jesus' citizenship as a man. Joseph and Mary, his parents, were Jews and from scripture we know Jesus was educated in the synagogue and travelled with his family to Jewish festivals and celebrations. Christians are grafted into this vine. Commencing with Abraham, who was accredited as 'righteous by faith with God' and from the patriarchs (Abraham, Isaac and Jacob) came the lineage of King David and the tribe of Benjamin, continuing to the birth of Christ. Through this mighty genealogy are the foundations of every Christian's citizenship and heritage.

Regrettably, it is mainly through the fortunes of war and the outcomes of military history that our world and economies are shaped. Kingdoms and empires rise and fall, changing the cultural landscapes, as people fleeing from conflict become displaced and refugees seek other countries for freedom and safety. Now, over fourteen hundred years later, after constant displacement throughout Europe, Jewry of every nationality have been returning to Israel in droves and Hebrew is again a national and first language.

Judaism's displacement was not only physical but spiritual.

Each life is a journey and gift to us by the living God with free will granted for the duration. Your decision to include Jesus on the journey, or should you choose to go it alone, will have vastly different outcomes in the present and in the future. Many people today are spiritually displaced even without being victims of vicious pogroms, persecution or in regions of conflict. From this observation, life is certainly no dress rehearsal – more of a rite of passage from the time we are born and commence the journey home. Every day carries a level of uncertainty and we need to remember who created us will also receive us. I was well on 'my way home' when a plane fell out of the sky with myself and four others in it.

Peace of mind was something I rarely experienced. With business pressure and day-to-day life, I was definitely displaced spiritually. Finding Jesus is the first step in building solid foundations for our journey. You only have to ask and when you do, you will be received unconditionally.

Starting on the road with the expanse of life to explore, you need someone to point out the signposts on the way. Knowledge and wisdom are required to travel safely and this particular journey being the most precious, as it is the gift of life. On every person's map of life, coloured by human experience, there will eventually be a distant point to conclude all you have ever done or been with your final journey home.

Paul, while in chains under the threat of Roman execution, wrote, *"I am torn between the two"* (*Philippians1:23 NIV*). Referring to his life in the spirit with Christ or to continuing his work while on earth. Even while displaced physically in some foul Roman prison, he was far from displaced in the spiritual, as His spiritual home was with Christ.

Paul's experience on the Road to Damascus was his crossroad. The real journey commenced after the scales fell from his eyes. Although he could see again physically and his heart was changed, fourteen years passed for the gradual transformation of Paul's mind. Constant guidance by the Holy Spirit during this period produced the greatest spokesperson for the New Testament and the planter of churches, in the known world, at that time.

We are all natural citizens of our land of birth. Paul was born in Tarsus, located in the province of Mersin in modern-day Turkey. He also retained Roman citizenship. God's family also has citizenship as a kingdom with guiding principles for each family member. Principles built around love and compassion with the Holy Spirit witnessing to our spirit and heritage for *"The Spirit himself testifies with our spirit that we are God's children" (Romans 8:16 NIV)* Since we are children of God, we have an inheritance a birthright and heritage, therefore we are heirs to His Kingdom.

Heirs do not exist unless there is an actual inheritance, for there is also a will, and someone needs to die for the will to become effective. Our physical circumstances, as with Paul in prison, are irrelevant, for in Jesus, we are not displaced spiritually.

Laws and regulations differ from nation to nation and like any citizen, you will have to familiarise yourself with them. In any new culture, you need to be aware of acceptable practices, things you can say and local colloquialisms should you offend someone. When you find Jesus, there are ten rules and one culture *"Love one another. As I have loved you, so you must love one another" (John 13:34 NIV).* All costs of your citizenship have been met by Jesus at the cross and entitlements are carefully written down: *"For I know the plans I have for you, declares the LORD, plans to prosper you and not harm you, plans to give you hope and a future" (Jeremiah 29:11 NIV).* Everything for the journey is there, from protection to provision and to promotion.

Citizens of his kingdom are transformed as seen with Paul and the disciples and other Christians of this world whose lives and spiritual home is in Jesus. You may have an external transformation when moving countries; many old ways of culture and thinking will still move with you. Some good and some not so good. Unlike the citizenship of Christ's Kingdom, where the transformation is internal with new paths laid before you.

When people meet Jesus, they are like the woman from Samaria, who drew water for Him. She was surprised the man resting by the well, obviously, a Jew, did not judge her. *"You are a Jew and I am a Samaritan woman. How can you ask me for a drink?" (For Jews did not associate with Samaritans)(John 4:9 NIV).* When Jesus revealed complete knowledge about her life the woman was amazed, *"Come, see a man who told me everything I ever did. Could this be the Messiah?" (John 4:29 NIV).* Is this a security and border control check before becoming a citizen? No, Jesus helped a woman with a past of multiple relationships understand that there would be security in Him. *"The woman said, I know that Messiah (called Christ) is coming. When he comes, he will explain everything to us. Then Jesus declared, I, the one speaking to you-I am He" (John 4:25–26 NIV).*

I was raised by Christian parents, and while in Jerusalem, I searched for Calvary and Christ's Tomb. At the time, due to the divided opinions within varying denominations on possible locations and my limited knowledge, none of my findings convinced me. Even so, Israel, in some way, still represented God to me and was a place of spiritual solace and kinship. Years later, I realised my search was of little importance as Christ is always present in the form of the Holy Spirit, the Counsellor, the Comforter. *"But the Advocate, the Holy Spirit, whom the Father will send in my name, will teach you all things and will remind of everything I have said to you"(John 14:26 NIV).*

Those who follow Jesus will know the power and presence of the Holy Spirit, the small, clear voice just one part of the inheritance. Life can present us with many unanswered questions and through the spirit we are taught and blessed with comfort and understanding. Jesus is constant and persevering; therefore, we need consistency in our reading of scripture, sharing prayers and building relationships with Him. Time spent in these endeavours will help you recognise the voice of the Holy Spirit, as millions of other Christians have. Most of this book originated through just this.

Approaching Jesus for the first time may seem daunting, very often pride can be holding people back. For some, it is not easy to review the balance sheet of life. A review will come eventually. Why not do it now?

Eye of the Spirit

"Time is a great teacher as long as we remain teachable."

EYE OF THE SPIRIT:

Sam is going grey around the ears and muzzle and a lot of water has gone under the bridge since he became part of the family. Time in the saddle is vital to any relationship and shared experiences are the cement and glue of friends. That cement forms spiritual bonds that are unbreakable.

Time is a great teacher as long as we remain teachable. Accepting the value of lessons learned and always seeking to grow. Better still, things forgotten are relived in our memory, being brought to our attention again. Our Lord reminded me to share the following, as the meaning is more relevant now than at the time when it occurred.

Sam and I encounter two hills on our walk, the second being the highest and steepest grades. As the hill levels out at the top, it develops into a shallow rise, ending as a cul-de-sac. On the property at the end of the cul-de-sac was an old tree with all the appearance of a cross, this being the focal point at the top of the hill before the return trip.

After numerous trips, I would see not a tree but a silvery cross with light pouring out of it and the more I looked it would shift in size. There came a certain day when Sam and I reached the hilltop and the tree was gone, finally cut down and removed. A small clear voice said, "You no longer need this. I am within you and the tree has been replaced."

This hill has always been a place of his presence and maybe you have had a location or special place where something similar has been experienced. From my understanding, the tree, a tangible thing, has been replaced fully by the spiritual. As *"Jesus resolutely set out for Jerusalem" (Luke 9:51 NIV),* we also need to fix our eye firmly on Jerusalem.

To acknowledge the existence of good and evil is also to accept that there is heaven and hell. As believers, to know there is a triune, is also to acknowledge the existence of the Holy Spirit, its power and presence. Comprehending this when things come against us, we can understand that they are in the spirit, even if expressed in the flesh. Battles will always exist, however, view the person or event not as the opponent but as a presence and attack on our spirit. Middle Eastern conflicts are spiritually founded, forcing Israel to battle with neighbouring nations most days. The foundations of these conflicts are spiritual and methods used for dealing with them are done in the flesh. Similarly, terrorism is the plague of the twenty-first century. Robbing western government economies and the world of stability. Due to its spiritual foundation, attempts to fight with the armour and sword of Saul, all will fall short compared to David's slingshot.

Therefore, realising the world is a place of conflict, it is essential we arm ourselves in the spirit.

Any believer who follows Jesus and reads scripture needs to seek God with the spirit, *"For we live (walk) by faith, not by sight" (2 Corinthians 5:7 NIV),* and faith is not blind. We become spiritually blind when we continue to consume what the world offers our spirit visually, *"But whenever anyone turns to the Lord, the veil is taken away" (2 Corinthians 3:16 NIV).*

As followers of Jesus, expectancy of the Holy Spirit's gifts should be second nature through faith. What is the point of faith if you are not expectant of what He can do in your life? For faith shows neither reluctance, nor is an act of duty, even if in the beginning it is something unseen and hope only. With faith and expectancy, we will change, so do not limit the good work and things Jesus wishes to share with you.

He says, "Be still, and know that I am God" (Psalm 46:10 NIV), a simple instruction so hard to undertake in the busyness of life. As *"My soul thirsts for God, for the living God. When can I go and meet with God?" (Psalm 42:2NIV)*, any time you choose to place other things on hold, and you set aside time to place Him first. Sam and I had times when the rain was not conducive to leaving the office, or business priorities appeared more important. We allow distractions and excuses to deprive us of so much. How can we expect a real leading of the spirit in our lives if time is not spent (not just at church) in His presence?

In 2012, Joshua Bell, violin virtuoso, was part of a Washington Post experiment. Dressed like any busker with a violin case open at his feet, he played in the subway for forty-five minutes, the violin used was a 3.5-million-dollar Stradivarius. Over one thousand people passed by Bell while he was playing; only seven stopped to listen, including a three-year-old boy and only one person recognised him. An opportunity to listen to one of the world's greatest violinists was missed, life's everyday distractions for the passers-by, simply all-consuming. Time has to be set aside to listen and experience a virtuoso like Joshua Bell to hear beautiful music that will touch the spirit. Time also needs to be set aside to spend with Jesus, so you experience the presence of the Holy Spirit. For none wish to *"Be ever hearing, but never understanding; be ever seeing, but never perceiving" (Isaiah 6:9 NIV).*

In time, we learn to know the small clear voice, through faith we gain spiritual sight and some day we may be told: "Seek me with the eyes of your spirit."

The Open Road

"…these unconditional acts of a few that choose to change the condition and lives of many."

THE OPEN ROAD:

On completion of this book, Sam and I will have covered more than 7000kms on the open road. Many pit stops and padding paws for Sam and several pairs of worn-out track shoes for me. My foundation for this book evolved from a desire to have a real relationship with my Father in Heaven, none of it happening overnight. Reading scriptures, prayer and rubber on the road were keys to knowing His voice. In a journey that could have taken you, as the crow flies, from Brisbane to Perth return, my wonderful four-legged friend Sam, has been my constant and loyal travelling companion.

As the Exodus took a million people from slavery to freedom and the Promised Land, they also left behind many ever-present masters to serve the one true master on their journey. To fulfil the dreams and aspirations of this life, we cannot be double minded as goals, due to our vacillation, will become watered down. A desire for all to prosper and to succeed is at the heart of God's will, as does any loving Father for his children. Very contrary to the schemes set by the world, which would have you serve them rather than they serve you. Don't forget your savings in a bank are a liability to the bank and your mortgage is an asset to them. Your indebtedness, if not careful, creates another master and who or what is that master like? Consider carefully the similarities to the oppression of the Egyptian masters and the subtlety of bondage in our everyday lives to consumerism.

Your exodus from your current life to a new life with God will not always be easy; you will still, as Moses was, be confronted with challenges. At the age of forty, Moses killed an Egyptian overseer who had brutalised one of his people. Aware his actions had become common knowledge, he fled from Egypt to the land of Midian, remaining there for forty years in self-inflicted exile. Moses' personal exodus commenced when all privileges of rank and wealth (which may have been binding) were shed. His journey's threshold with God, now far removed from the affluent quarters of the palace. During this period, God groomed and prepared him to lead His chosen people out of Egypt, thereby laying the cornerstone for the Israelite nation. Moses, a reluctant and inexperienced leader with a speech impediment, set in motion the Exodus at eighty years of age. Making a logistical nightmare materialize through God's mighty power.

Knowing someone has your back every day is an incredible blessing and spiritually freeing. As God was with Moses, the same applies to you and me. My exodus was not overnight; it commenced with a near disaster and through a miracle, I am still here. Ever since life has been a process of adjustment and pruning, removing old habits, all required to reshape the vine of my life.

Learning to live this life to the fullest and to be a free man or woman comes when we let Jesus answer the questions. His admonishment is done with love, for He was and still is an inconvenient truth, *"But he was pierced for our transgressions, he was crushed for our iniquities;" (Isaiah 53:5 NIV)*.

For years, I struggled with an 'A' type personality and I am certain others have experienced the poor fruit it can produce. However, our Heavenly Father is our 'Father', and He has no desire for his children to live like this. Our spirit is neither up for grabs nor to be stolen, with our purpose and value removed, never His intention. Nor were we and our families to be bound and held captive to the inclinations and the ways of the world.

The purpose, significance and value of all men and women lie in Jesus. He is the man in the boy and the woman in the girl. Christ is the true source of moral and spiritual fibre to be distributed to those around you at work and home. Paul expressed just this when he wrote:

"What is more, I consider everything a loss because of the surpassing worth of knowing Christ Jesus my Lord, for whose sake I have lost all things. I consider them garbage, that I may gain Christ" (Philippians 3:8 NIV).

On another note, the reasons and criticisms raised for choosing not to attend a church can vary greatly and one I recently heard concerned tithing and money. Desiring to serve Him mind, body and spirit means we can only serve one God. A personal act of tithing expresses obedience and generosity, recognising God as the source of our provision, as already mentioned he is the foundation of all things. Your ability and desire to accumulate is neither the issue nor the concern. His proviso being, place Him first *"you shall have no other gods before me" (Exodus 20:3 NIV)*. If you are blessed with the mindset and skills to create wealth, do not forget God's Kingdom, and his desire to know you, remembering the blessings He bestows each day.

We are guaranteed to leave this world as every living thing does. Our day, hour or place and location is unknown. Regardless of all the experiments by science to clone and develop immortality, let us accept through the evidence of design that there is a creator. When we look around us at our children, wildlife, cosmos and even Sam, life forms are all interlaced. A tapestry so complex and remarkable in structure, there must be a designer. Abraham was told as the father of all nations:

"I will surely bless you and make your descendants as numerous as the stars in the sky and as the sand on the seashore." (Genesis 22:17 NIV)

On a crisp, cold night when you look to the heavens, stars that you see are being compared in number to grains of sand on the shores of the world. Four thousand years later, science has confirmed they believe this to be true.

Anyone who truly loves you, will place you before themselves and does not demand that you love them. Parents will do anything for their children in the realm of what they know is best for them. With this in mind, God surrendered his Son as the only possible way to replace the old covenant with a better one. I have often wondered at God's sorrow for His

Son's terrible suffering so we as His children could be gathered to Him.

The New Covenant is a gift of unconditional love; come as you are recognising my Son and what he has done for you. A covenant is not a contract where explicit conditions, governed by the laws of a nation, meet the requirements of separate parties. Many contracts contain loopholes for the unwary and are only as good as the honesty of the signatories. For Jesus came to complete the law (the Old Covenant) first for the Jew and then the Gentile replacing atonement with forgiveness. God's covenant with the world is something He has to fulfil, a pledge, giving of oneself (His Son) for the other (you). We are not forced to honour this covenant due to the freedom of choice and the fulfilment of His pledge by his Son, Jesus:

"For God so loved the world he gave his one and only Son, that whoever believes in him shall not perish but have eternal life." (John 3:16 NIV)

How can you and I see *The Open Road*, or should I say, how do you and I identify *The Open Road*? We will find this through the lens of scripture, God's grace, and the companionship of the Holy Spirit. We can also observe it in mankind's struggle for freedom in the face of adversity. Ships that cross oceans, taking medical care and the Gospel to people of undeveloped nations. Through the courage and convictions of men and women, who risk all to protect the persecuted and vulnerable. You will see it in a young man helping the elderly across the road, in situations of selflessness, so others are blessed and upheld.

All these unconditional acts of a few choose to change the condition and lives of many.

You will climb mountains on *The Open Road*, personal mountains. There will also be deserts, but sometimes those places of isolation are good, utilised as times for considerable learning. When you cross them, do look carefully. You will find clear living water, the essence of who you are, as Isaiah wrote:

"See, I am doing a new thing! Now it springs up; do you not perceive it? I am making a way in the wilderness and streams in the wasteland." (Isaiah 43:19 NIV)

The Open Road, although not wide, will seem infinite. There are no strangers on it, and God's Son, whom you meet, knows you better than you know yourself.

Michael and Sam

Epilogue

You have wandered through heavenly pastures filled with excellent things.

Seeking truth and understanding.

My hand will always be upon you, not lifted or taken from your shoulder.

I will gently guide you in the paths of righteousness.

My blessings will not be taken from you.

For all earthly things will fade and perish, my presence will always be with you.

You say who am I to write this, is this the word of God?

It is the prompting of the Holy Spirit.

Some say faith is hope you now say faith is trust.

Why, because you know Me.

For have I not told you very excellent things,

For have I not been present at every point in your mind when you write?

For I am God, I am Creation,

I am the Son of the Highest who gathers my Father's family to him.

Whispers and rumours of difficult times will come like a plague.

It will be a swarm like locusts disturbing the nations of this world.

Uncertainty is not My name, it belongs to another.

Fear is not My name, neither is doubt or deceit.

For as you know, I am a loving Father for all mankind.

Bibliography

Page 22: *A very clever television advertisement……...when we could pass the glory to others.* Westpac Australia, produced by DDB Advertising.

Page 25-26: *Some time back, I was given a book…………other interests in life.*
Iacocca: an autobiography published 1984 by Lee Iacocca and William Novak (Bantam Dell Publish Group)

Page30: *Alpha Course*
(https://alpha.org-nickey-gumbel)https://alpha.orgs

Page 35: *The Lady of the Lamp*
Wikipedia.

Page37: *'Your mission should you choose to accept it'.*
TV Series Mission Impossible.

Page 40: *A young Christian woman, Bethany Hamilton lost her arm in shark attack while surfing.*
Wikipedia.

Page 40: *'I have missed more than 9000 shots in my career……. .that is why I succeed.' Michael Jordan.*
Brainy Quote.

Page 41: *'I have not failed but found 10000 ways that don't work' Thomas Edison.*
Brainy Quote.

Page 41: *The Man in the Arena – Theodore Roosevelt.*
From Theodore Roosevelt's' Citizen in the Republic, Paris address 1910

Page 43: *'Courage is rightly considered the foremost of the virtues, for upon it all others depend' Winston Churchill.*
Quotetab.

Page 50-51: *Operating under forty percent power……. even at the risk of his own life – Charlie Brown and Franz Stigler WWII Incident.*
Wikipedia.

Page63: *'The secret is not to focus all your energy on fighting the old but fighting the new.'*
Socrates – Online Socrates Quotes

Page71: *'We are more than flesh and bones……..and yet it is there' Dr.Ben Carson.*
WhatshouldIreadnext.com

Page 71: *The first ever marathon runner was a guy by the name of Pheidippides around 490BC.*

Wikipedia.

Page 82-83: *The Bridge of Spies – 2015 film directed by Steven Spielberg*
Additional information Wikipedia.

Page 88: *'Hardships often prepare ordinary people for an extraordinary destiny'.*
C.S. Lewis

Page 90: *'I believe God made me for a purpose, but he also made me fast, and when I run, I feel his pleasure' Eric Liddell.*
1981 Film Chariots of Fire, directed by Hugh Hudson.

Page 119:*The society which scorns excellence……pipes nor theories will hold water.'*
John W Gardner.

Page 129: *'Climbing is always intentional at the very least.'*
John C. Maxwell

Page 129: *Televised interview conducted by Canon J Johns with Lord Michael Hastings* – Facing the Canon.

Page 129: *'We, ourselves, feel that what we are doing is just a drop in the ocean but the ocean would be less for that drop' Mother Teresa.*

Mother Teresa received the Nobel Peace Prize in 1979, died 1997 and was beatified October 2003.

Page 135: *'A war of extermination and massacre'* Abul Rahman Hassan Azzam, the Secretary General of the Arab League 1947.

Also known as the Azzam Pasha quotation and was universally sited for decades as having been uttered at the outbreak of hostilities between Arab states and Israel months later.

Wikipedia.

Page147: *Relationships require all parties to walk shoulder to shoulder sharing successes and failures.* John C. Maxwell.

Page147: *'In fact, I was assuming that the human mind is completely ruled by reason. But that is not so.'* C.S. Lewis – Mere Christianity, chapter 12.

Page158: *Three Bedouin shepherds in late 1946 early 1947* Internet searched for information.

Page 161: *'I forgive you brother with all my heart.'* Corrie Ten Boom.
Faith Gateway article July 24th 2019

Page166: *Epicentre* – Joel Rosenberg, published August 2006

Page171: *Eliyahu Asher, 25th June 2006*
Israel National News 215215-Benny Toker 19th July 2016

Page187: *Joshua Bell*
Youtube-Washington Post Subway Experiment, Washington DC Union Station 2007